TIRUKKAḺUKKUṈṞAM

(Pakṣitīrtham)

AND ITS TEMPLES

(A Study of their History, Art and Architecture)

TIRUKKAḺUKKUṈṞAM
(Pakṣitīrtham)
AND ITS TEMPLES

(A Study of their History, Art and Architecture)

K.V. GOPALAKRISHNAN

abhinav publications

Cataloging in Publication Data--DK
Courtesy: D.K. Agencies (P) Ltd. <docinfo@dkagencies.com

Rajam, K.V. (Kadayam Venkatram), 1936-
Tirukkalukkunram (Pakshitirtham) and its temples:
a study of their history, art and architecture / K.V. Rajam.
p. cm.
Originally presented as the author's (M.Litt.)
-- University of Madras.
Includes bibliographical references (p.)
Includes Index.
ISBN 8170173922

1. Temples, Hindu--India--Tirukkalukkunram--History. 2. Architecture, Hindu--India--Tirukkalukkunram--History. I. Title.

DDC 294.535 095 482 21

First published in India 2005

Publishers
Shakti Malik
Abhinav Publications
E-37 Hauz Khas
New Delhi-110016 (INDIA)
Phones: 26566387, 26562784, 26524658
Fax: 91-11-26857009
e-mail: shakti@nde.vsnl.net.in
website: http://www.abhinavexports.com

ISBN 81-7017-392-2

Lasertypeset by
Onkar Digital Studio
Rohini, Delhi

Printed at
D.K. Fine Art Press Pvt. Ltd.
Ashok Vihar, Delhi

CONTENTS

PREFACE

The present work is based on my research work (for two years 1958-60) on the subject for M.Litt. degree in the Department of Indian History and Archaeology, University of Madras. I am thankful to the University for permitting its publication.

I acknowledge my deep sense of gratitude to my esteemed teachers. Dr. T.V. Mahalingam, Dr. K.K. Pillay and Dr. M. Arokiaswami, former Professors of Indian History in the University of Madras for their valuable guidance and advice.

I thank the Archaeological Survey of India and especially the Chief Epigraphist for providing access to the unpublished inscriptions and supplying a few photographs. My thanks are also due to Mr. Patrick Gassie of Boulogne, France and the H.R. & C.E. Department, Tamilnadu for lending me a number of photographs included in the volume.

My hearty thanks are due to my parents K.V. Parthasarathi Iyengar and Smt. Janaki and my wife, Smt. Rajam for their encouragement and support. I should record my special sense of gratitude to my elder brother, Dr. K.V. Raman, former Professor of Archaeology, University of Madras for his guidance and the keen interest in my work. I thank Shri Shakti Malik of Abhinav Publications, New Delhi for publishing the volume so well.

K.V. GOPALAKRISHNAN

LIST OF ILLUSTRATIONS

ABBREVIATIONS

A.R.E.	*Annual Report of Epigraphy*
E.I.	*Epigraphia Indica*
I.A.	*Indian Antiquary*
J.I.H.	*Journal of Indian History*
M.J.L.S.	*Madras Journal of Literature and Science*
S.I.T.I.	*South Indian Temple Inscriptions*

PLANS

G.P. I	*General Plan of Orukal Mandapa*
G.P. II	*General Plan of Bhaktavatsala Temple*

INTRODUCTION

This work presents a historical study of an important pilgrim-centre of South India namely Tirukkaḻukkuṉṟam, also known as Pakṣitīrtham or "Sacred eagle hill". The importance of the study of local history in a vast country like India need hardly be emphasized. Particularly South India, where there are numerous temples of great antiquity, affords a fertile field for research into local history. Often, these temples have gone through a long evolutionary process, documenting, as it were, the history of the locality and the activities of the people therein, through the ages. Inscriptions found in the temples are valuable source of information for the historical vicissitudes through which the locality passed. They also throw much light on the religious, economic and social life of the people of the locality. It is well-known that in South India the temples were important centres of cultural and social life. Their importance extended beyond the purely religious and spiritual realms. They were indeed the nucleus round which the village developed and the hub of all activities, social, economic and artistic. A study of architecture of such temples is also very revealing. Often, the temple-complex, as is present, today, is the product of centuries of growth and evolution. The various structures of the temple were added to the main shrine by stages. A close study of the architectural features of the structures gives us an insight into the different styles, prevalent in different times. Artistic excellence reached by the ancient people of the locality is also borne out by the sculptures and bronze images in the temples.

These facts amply illustrate the importance of temples in the study of local history. Tirukkaḻukkuṉṟam is no exception to this general rule. It contains three ancient and venerable temples which in many ways symbolise the religion, art and culture of the area. Though, politically, Tirukkaḷukkuṉṟam was of no particular importance, yet by virtue of its situation between the capital city of Kāñci and the chief port of Māmallapuram, it has received the patronage of Pallava Kings. The inscriptions found in the temples of Tirukkaḷukkuṉṟam belong to many a dynasty like the Pallava, Chōḷa, Raṣṭrakuṭa, Pāṇḍya, Vijayanagara, Kāḍavarāyas and Śambuvarāyas. This clearly shows the many-sided political vicissitudes through which this place had passed.

The influence of the temples over the place in its economic and social life is striking. They have played the role of an employer, consumer, landlord, an educational centre and a centre of culture and, to a great extent, shaped the economic and social life of the people.

The role of the temples in the religious history of the place is also of great interest. Throughout the eventful history, Tirukkaḷukkuṉṟam has remained an active centre of Śaivism and the great Nāyanmārs of Tēvāram fame were associated with the place. Other great Śaiva apostles like Māṇikkavācakar, Paṭṭinattu Aḍigaḷ, Aruṇagirināthar visited the place and were greatly inspired by it. The place is also rich in religious traditions and practices which have made it an important holy place of South India. Most remarkable, is the regular visit of two eagles at about 11 a.m. every day to the Vedagiri Hill to take the sacred food offering *prasādam*. Hence the name Pakṣitīrtham. According to popular tradition, this practice has been going on for ages. People from all over India and abroad visit this place to see this wonderful sight. Added to this, is the importance of the Sankutīrtham where a conch is said to be 'born' once in twelve years. This is a unique occasion which draws thousands of people. Many other traditions and festivals have made this place worthy of study from the point of view of religious and social history of this place.

From the architectural point of view, Tirukkaḷukkuṉṟam is also of considerable interest and importance. The Ōrukal Mandapa, the rock-cut temple half-way up the hill was the creation of the illustrious Pallava King Narasimhavarma I or Māmalla of Māmallapuram fame. The hill temple for

Vēdagirīśvara, eulogised by the Tevaram hymners and other saints, also has many architectural features of the Pallava period. Down the hill, in the heart of the town is the large and magnificent temple complex of Bhaktavatsala with impressive gopuras or the four gateways in four cardinal directions besides beautiful sub-shrines and multi-columned halls (*mandapas*). We also have here representations of other styles of Dravidian architecture — early Cōḷa, late Cōḷa, Vijayanagara and post-Vijayanagara — which afford ample scope for the study of architectural evolution at the place. The temples of Tirukkaḻukkuṉṟam also contain remarkable sculptures and bronze-images of rare beauty and symbolism which deserve a detailed study.

Sources for writing the history of Tirukkaḻukkuṉṟam and its temples are many. Traditions, literature, religious and secular, inscriptions and architectural evidences, which are set out in detail in the Appendices of the thesis, come to our help.

Chapter 1

TOPOGRAPHY, PLACE NAME AND ARCHAEOLOGY

LOCATION

Tirukkaḷukkuṉṟam (the sacred hill of the eagles) or Pakṣitīrtham in Sanskrit lies about nine miles west of Mahābalipuram or Māmallapuram, the well-known ancient port and art centre of the Pallavas of Kāñci. It lies also nine miles south-east of Chingleput on the Southern route. Sadras, the old Dutch settlement on the east coast, is nine miles south-east of Tirukkaḷukkuṉṟam. The place lies very near the Pālār basin, a little away from Vāyalūr, where the river Pālār empties itself into the sea. Tirukkaḷukkuṉṟam is in the Chingleput taluk, in Chingleput district, in Tamilnadu. There is a good motorable road from Madras to Tirukkaḷukkuṉṟam passing through Chingleput. There is also the coastal road to the place from Madras via Māmallapuram. The present Chingleput district as a whole formed part of the ancient territorial division called Toṇḍaimaṇḍalam.[1]

TOPOGRAPHY

The topographical features of the region round Tirukkaḷukkuṉṟam are simple. The ground rises gradually

1. From epigraphical sources it is known that Toṇḍaimaṇḍalam was divided into twenty-four kōṭṭams. About twelve kōṭṭams lay within the limits of the modern district of Chingleput. Tirukkaḷukkuṉṟam formed part of the Kaḷattūrkōṭṭam.

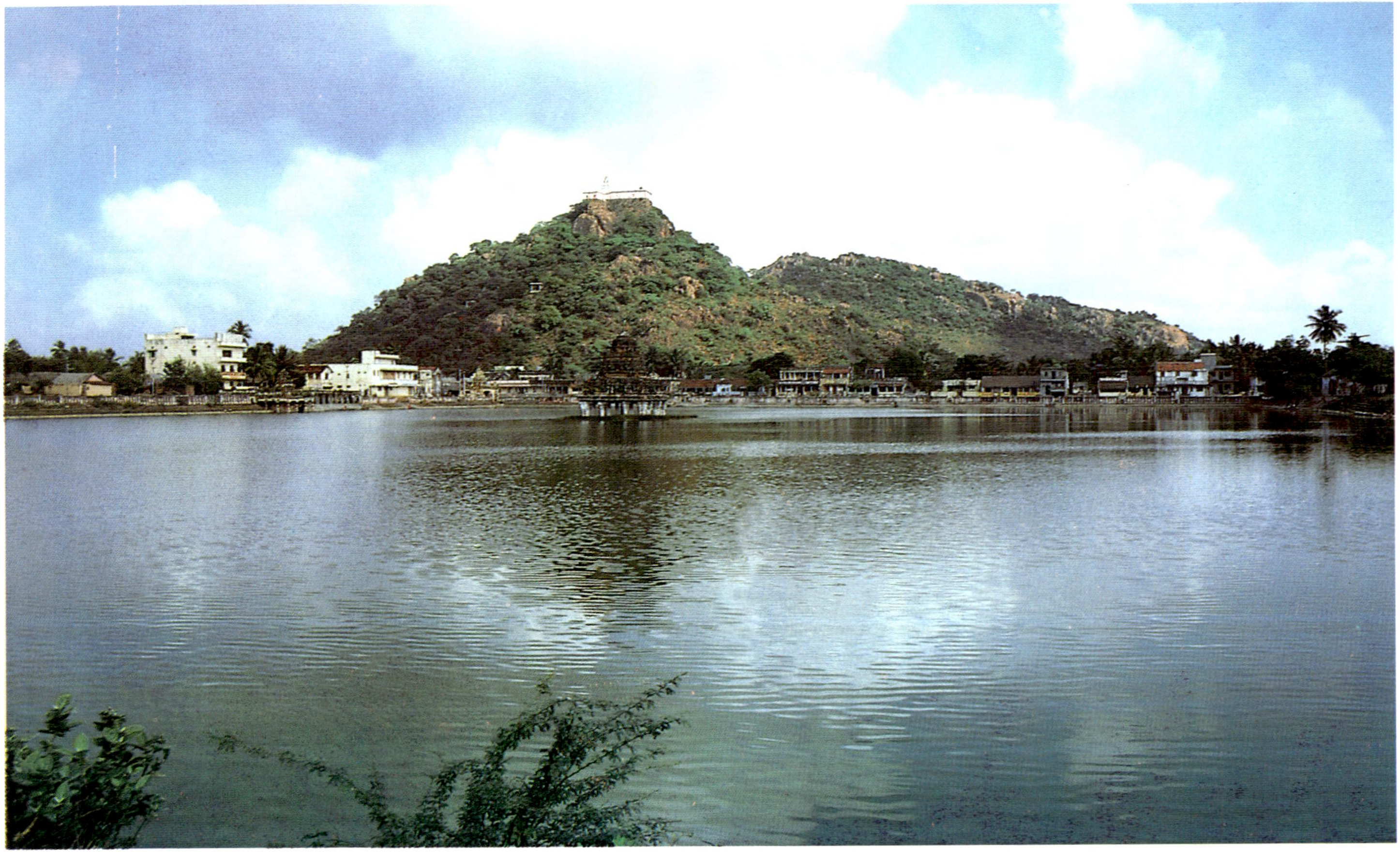

Fig. 1 Vēdagiri Hill and Sanku Tīrtham Tank

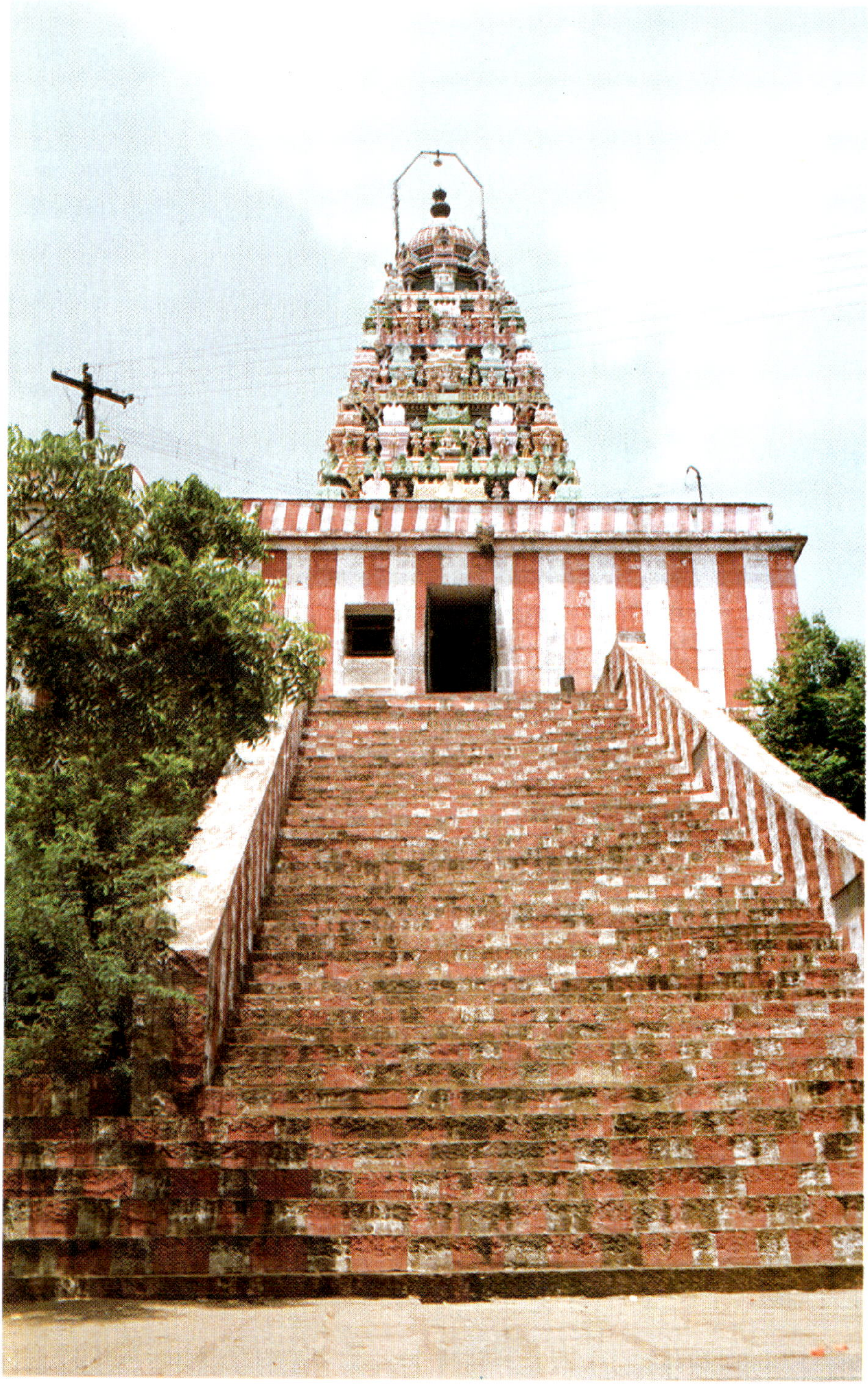

Fig. 2 Vēdagirīśvara temple - Close view

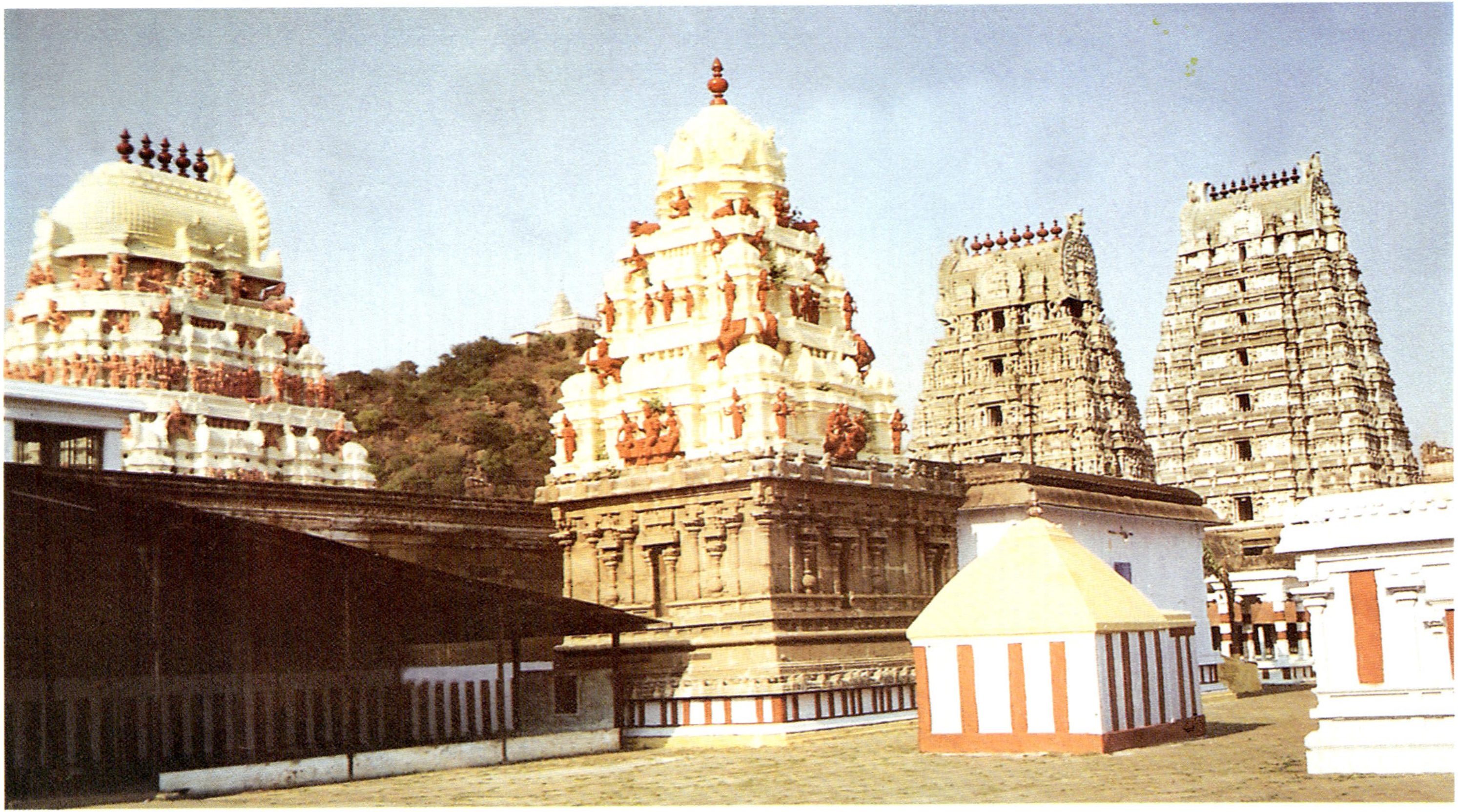

Fig. 10 Shrines of Bhaktavatsala (left) and Vēdagirīśvara Utsavamūrti (right)

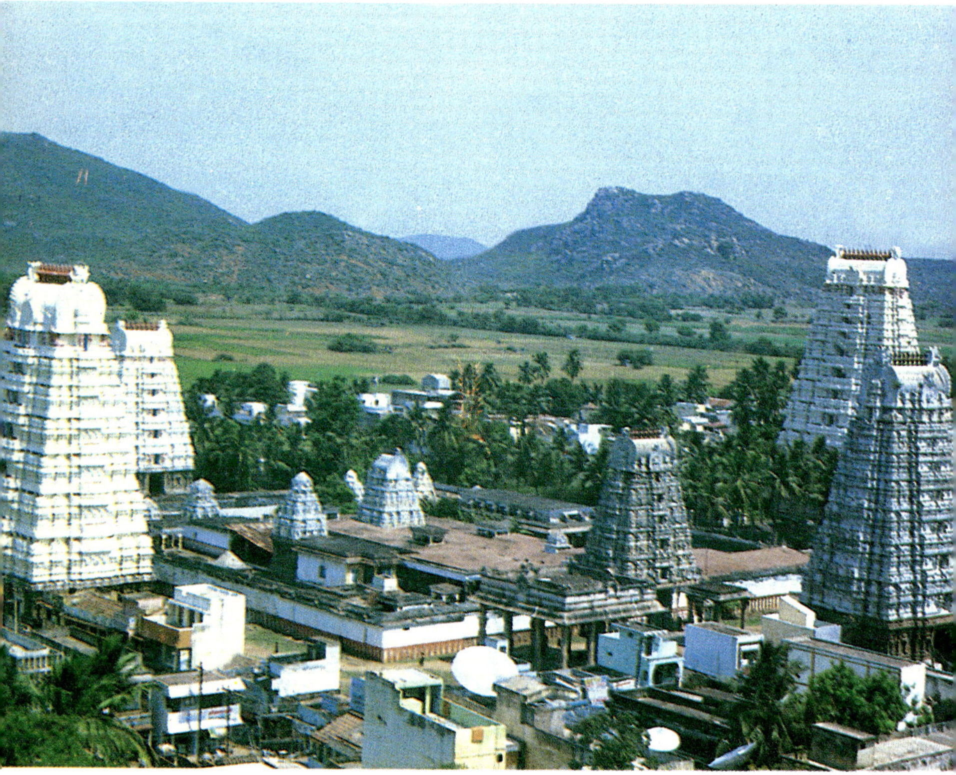

Fig. 4 Panoramic view of the Bhaktavatsala Temple

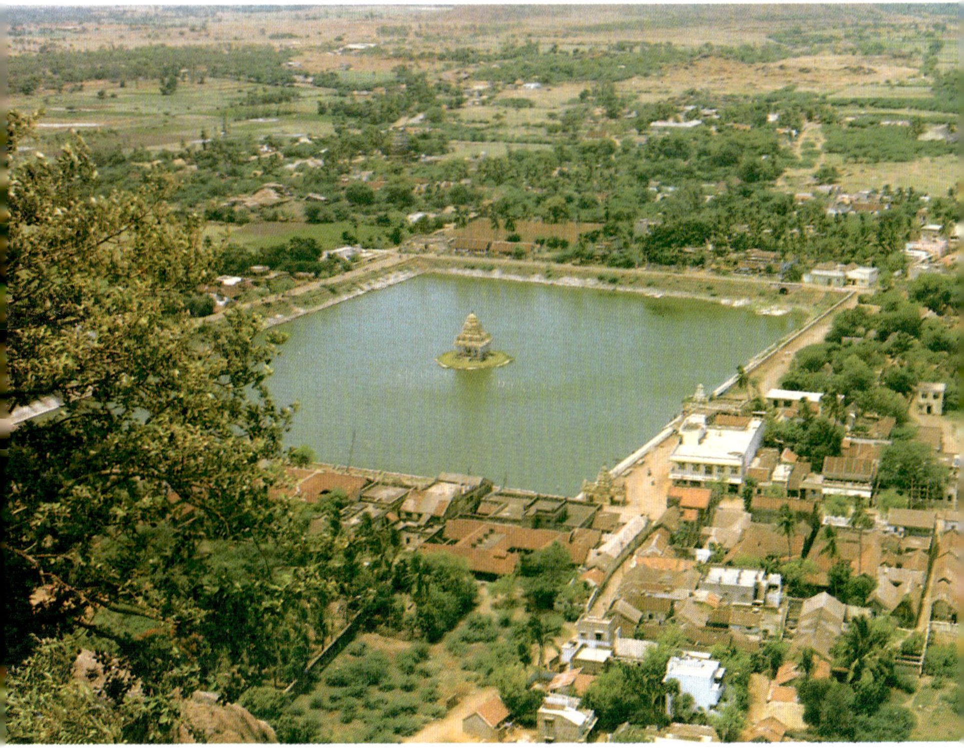

Fig. 5 Sanku Tīrtham Tank

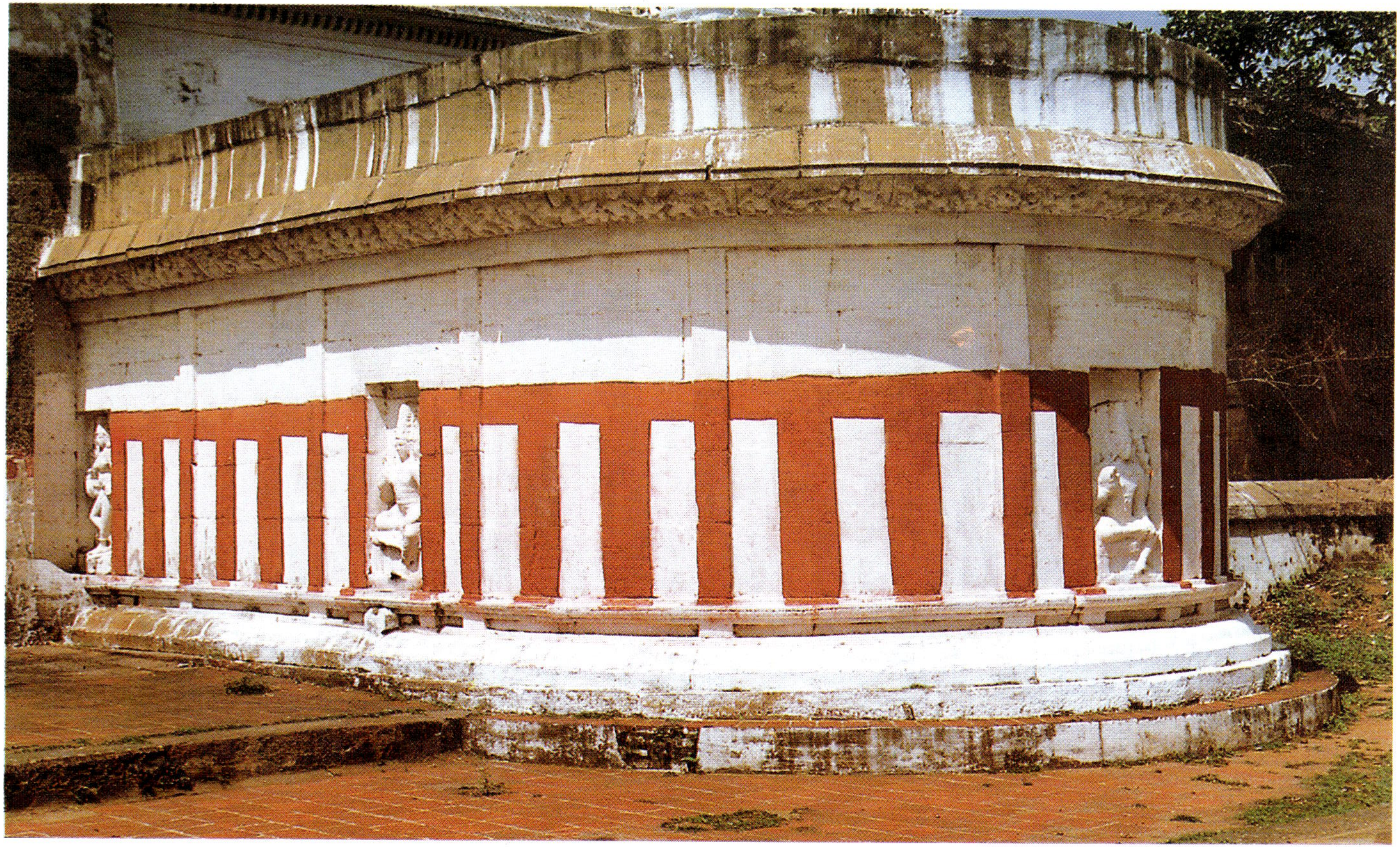

Fig. 11 Tiruābharaṇa Koṭṭaḍi (apsidal shrine)

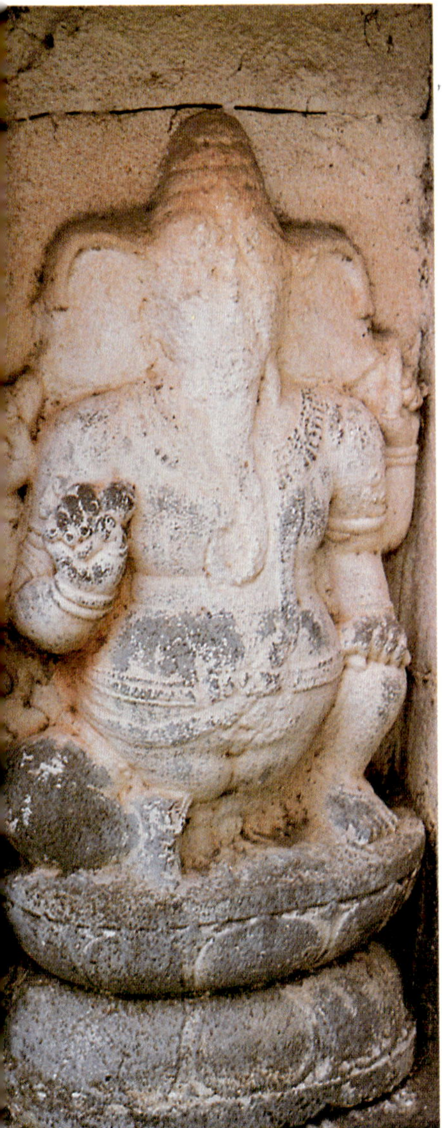

Fig. 12 Gaṇeśa

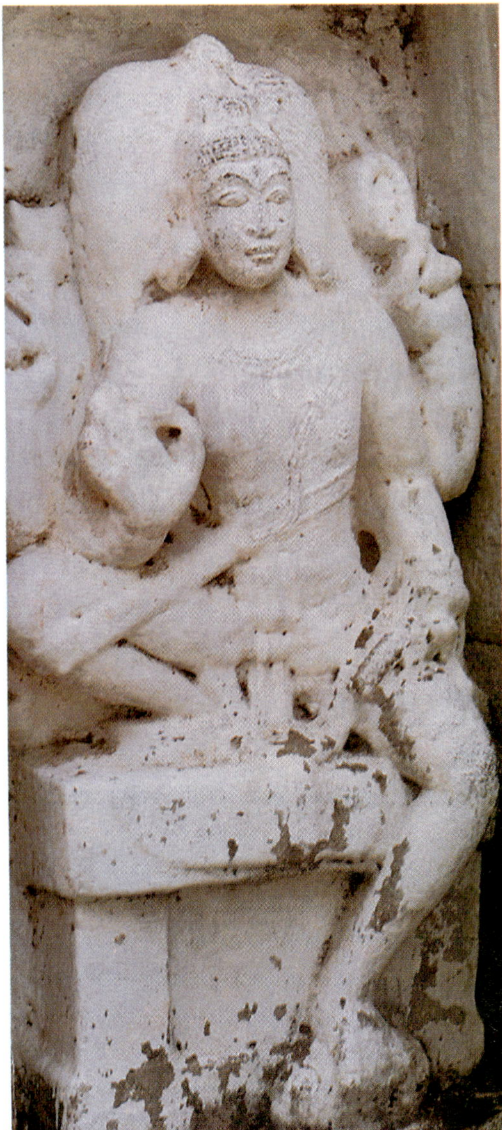

Fig. 13 Dakṣiṇāmūrti

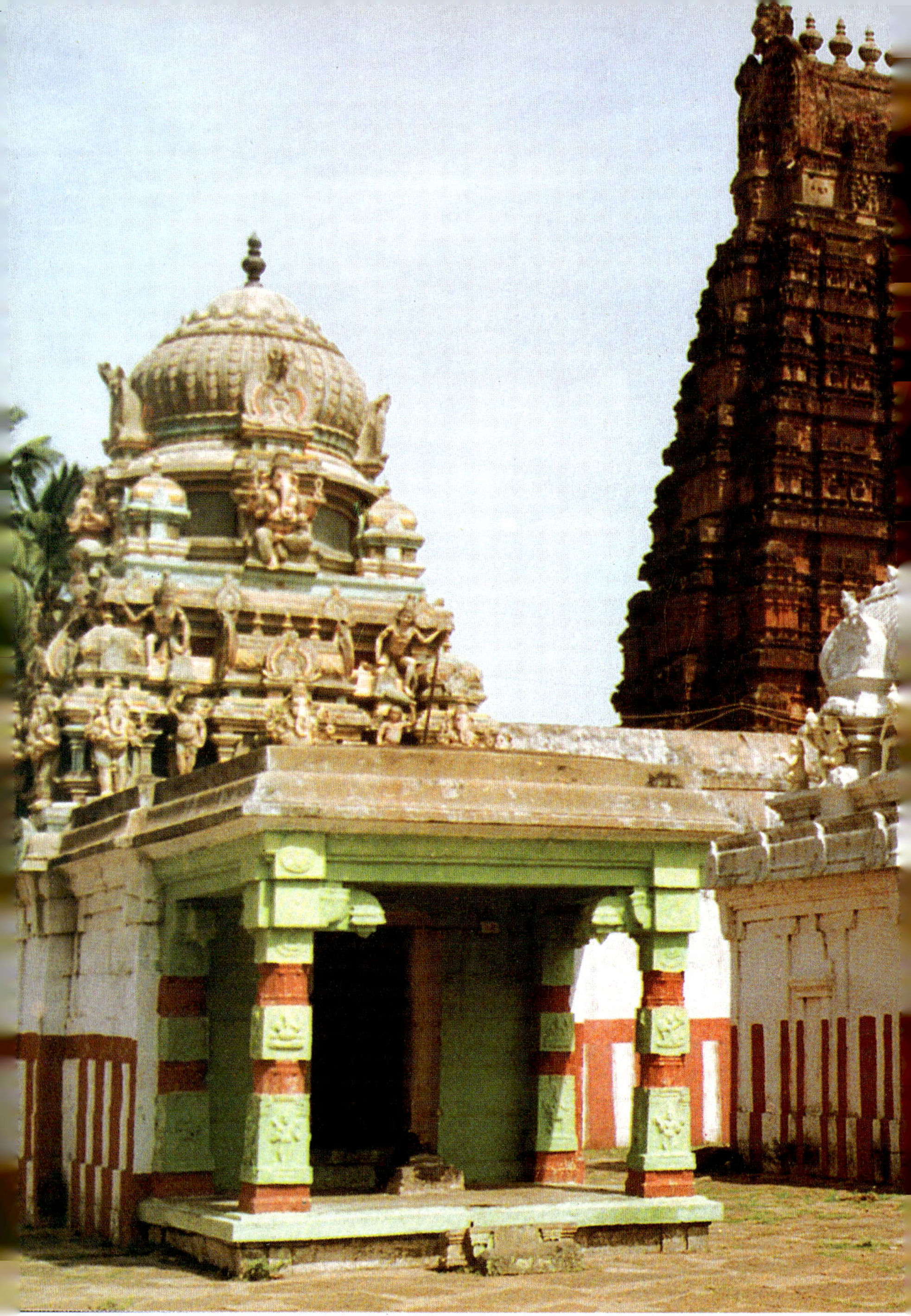

Fig. 19 Shrine of Vaṇḍuvana Piḷḷaiyār (left) and Jambukēśvara (centre) and Subrahmaṇya (right)

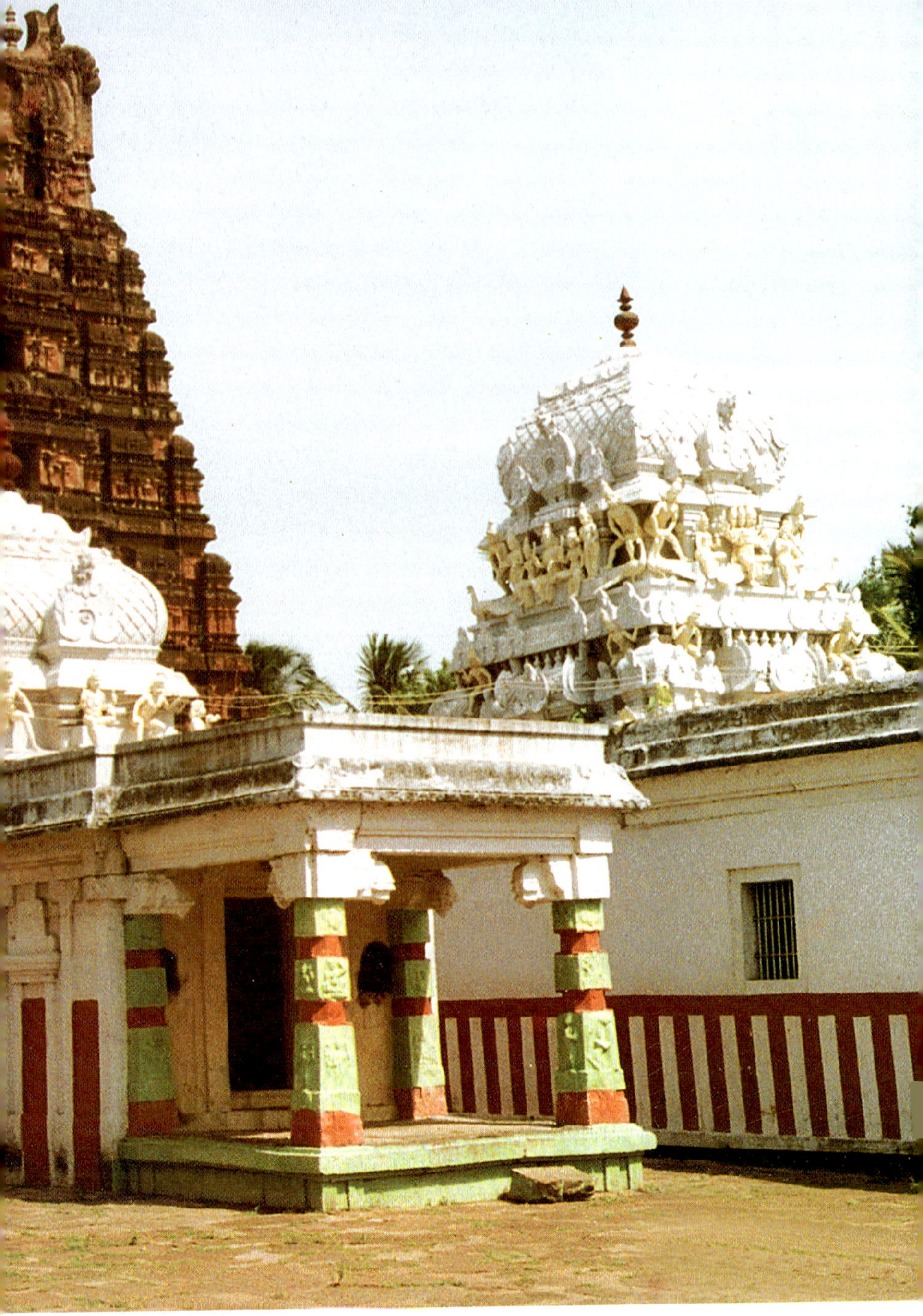

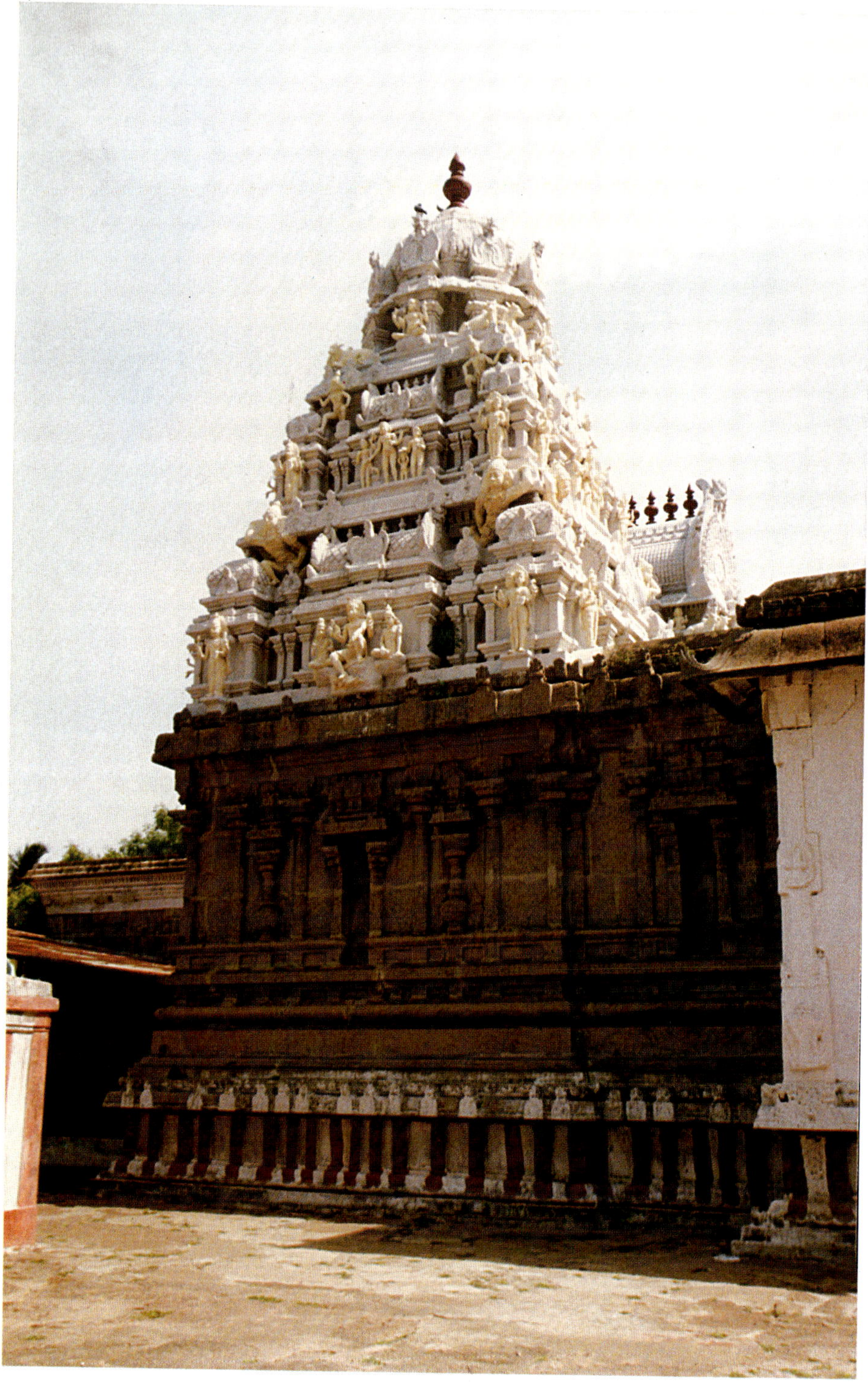

Fig. 18 Vēdagirīśvara Shrine (Utsavamūrti)

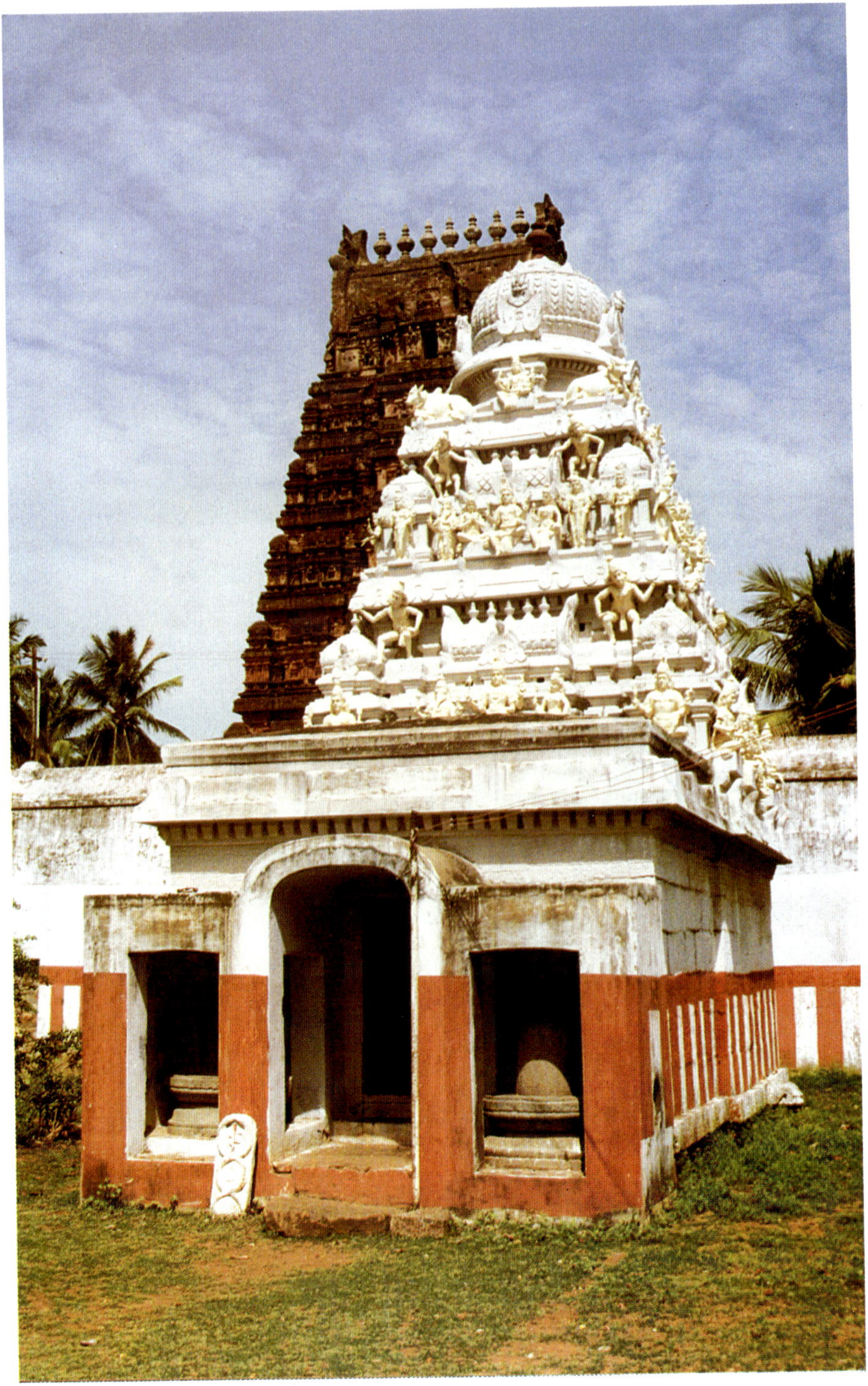

Fig. 20 Arunācalēśvara Shrine

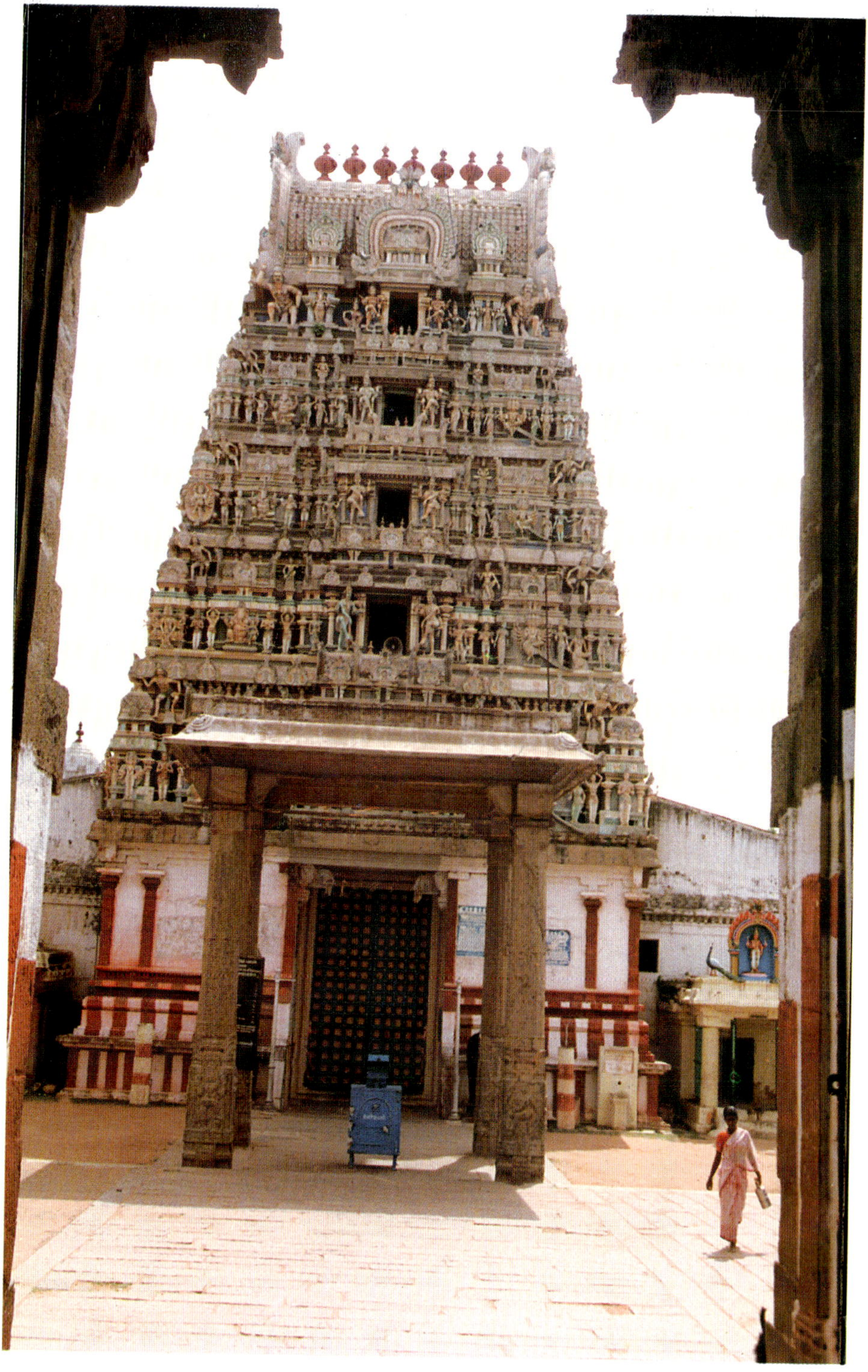

Fig. 21 Riṣi Gōpura

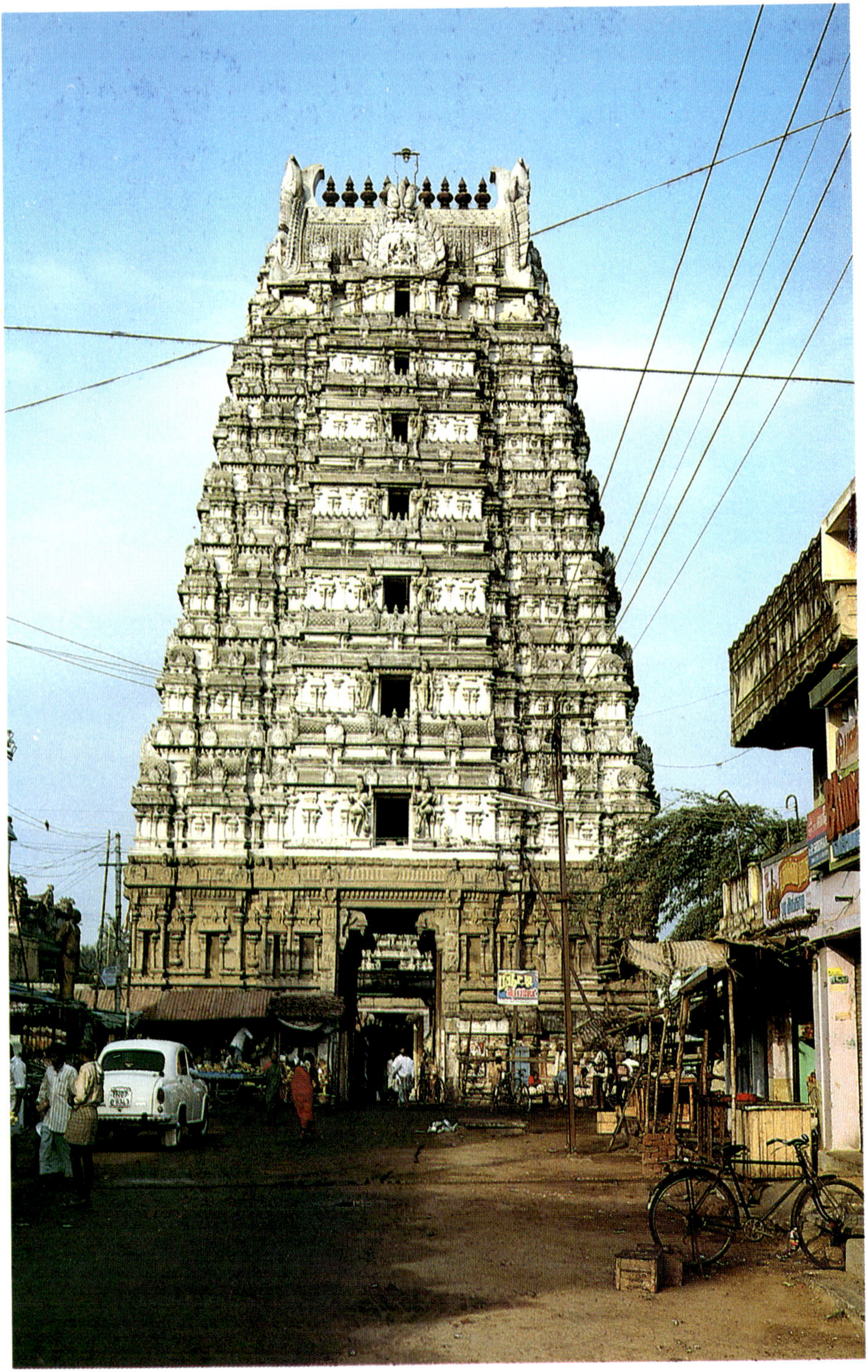

Fig. 22 Eastern Gōpura

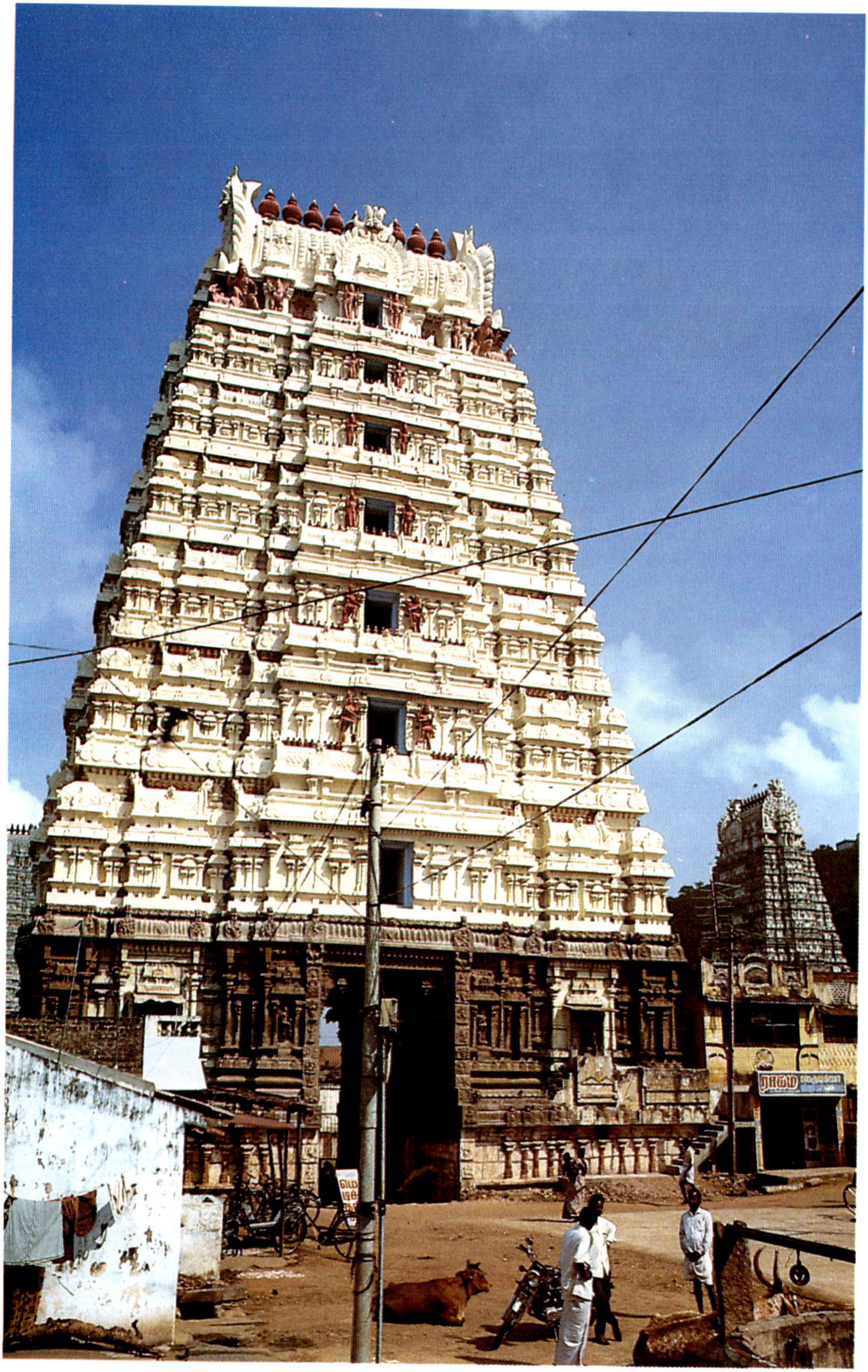

Fig. 23 Southern Gōpura

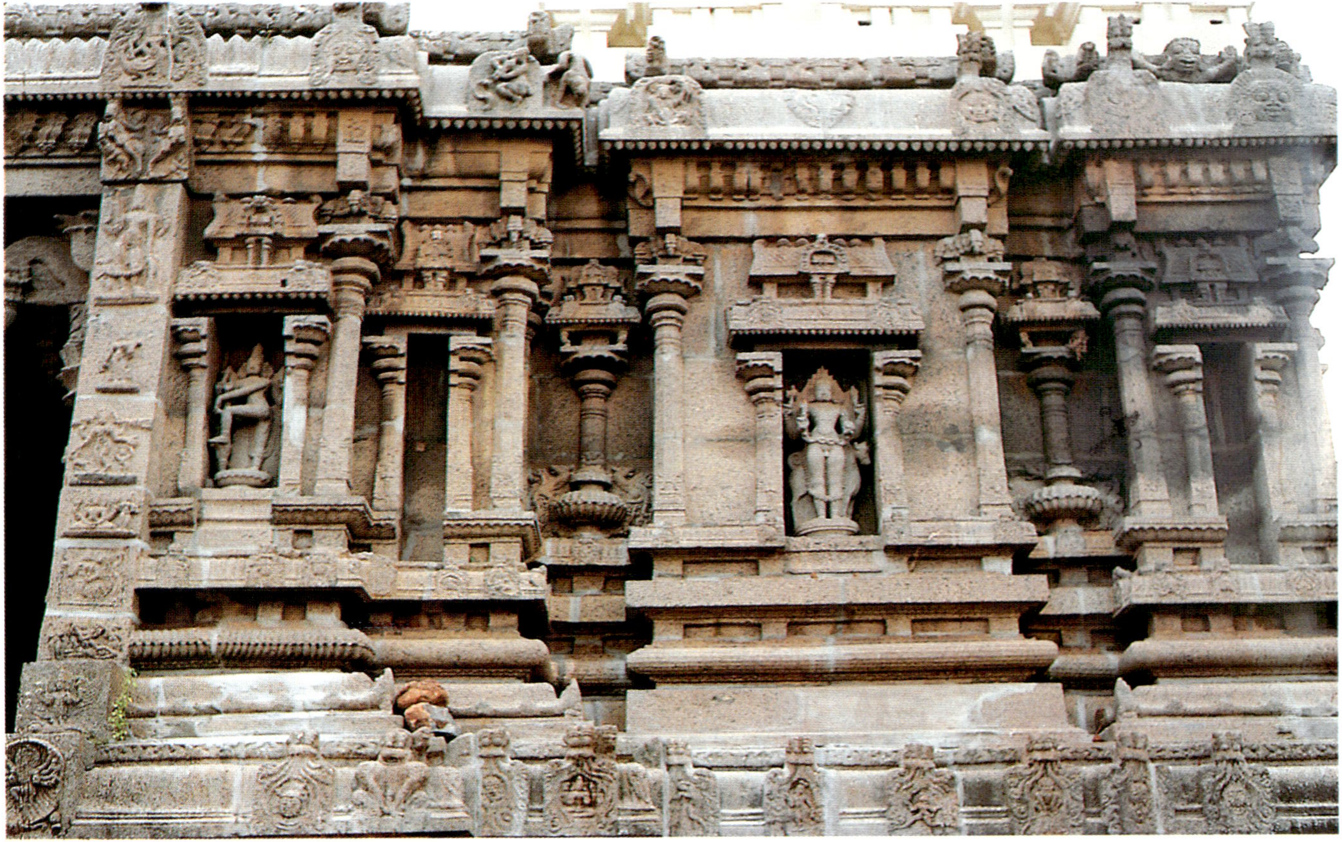

Fig. 24 Southern Gōpura (details of plinth)

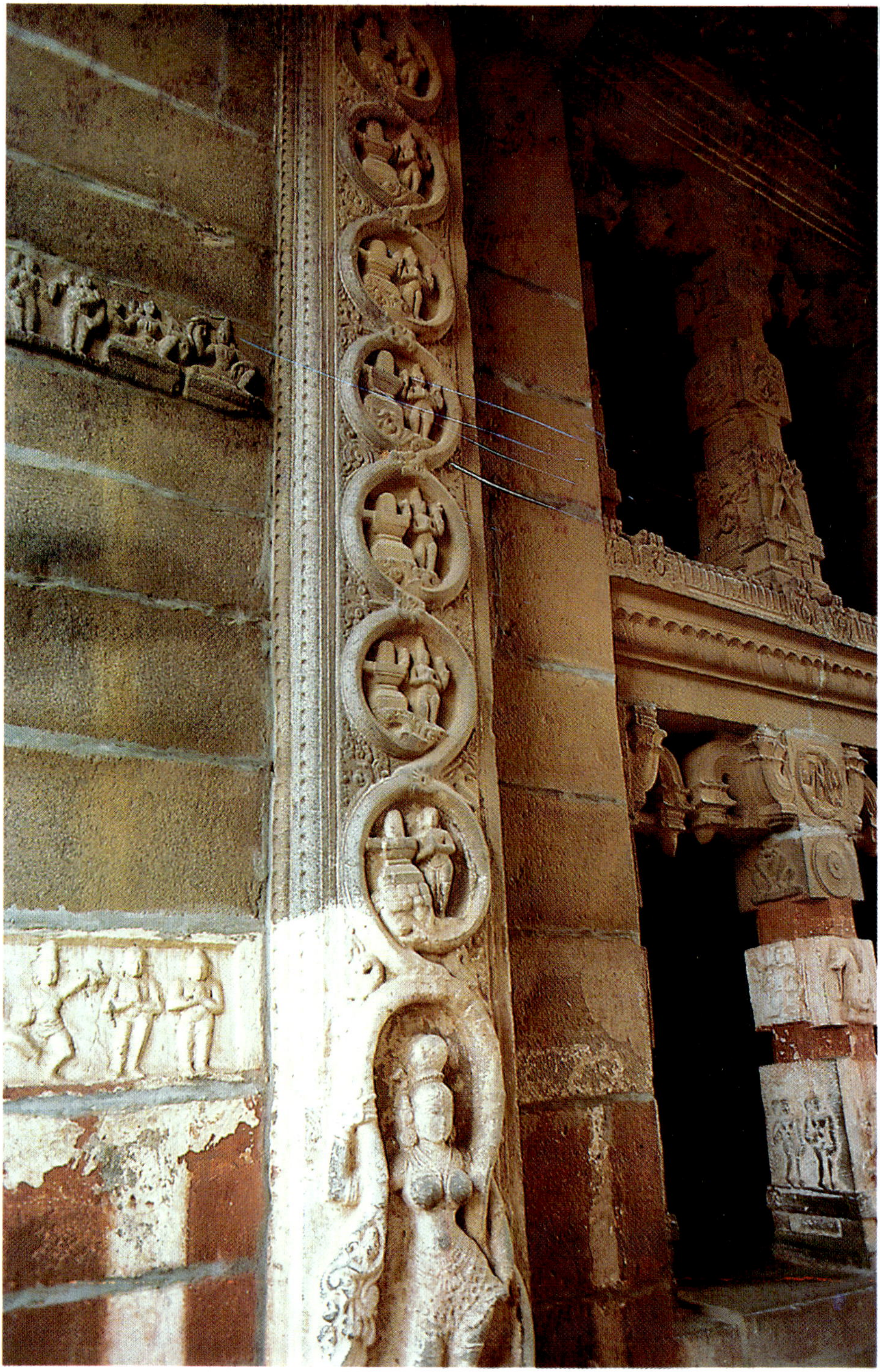

Fig. 25 Entrance Doorway of Southern Gōpura

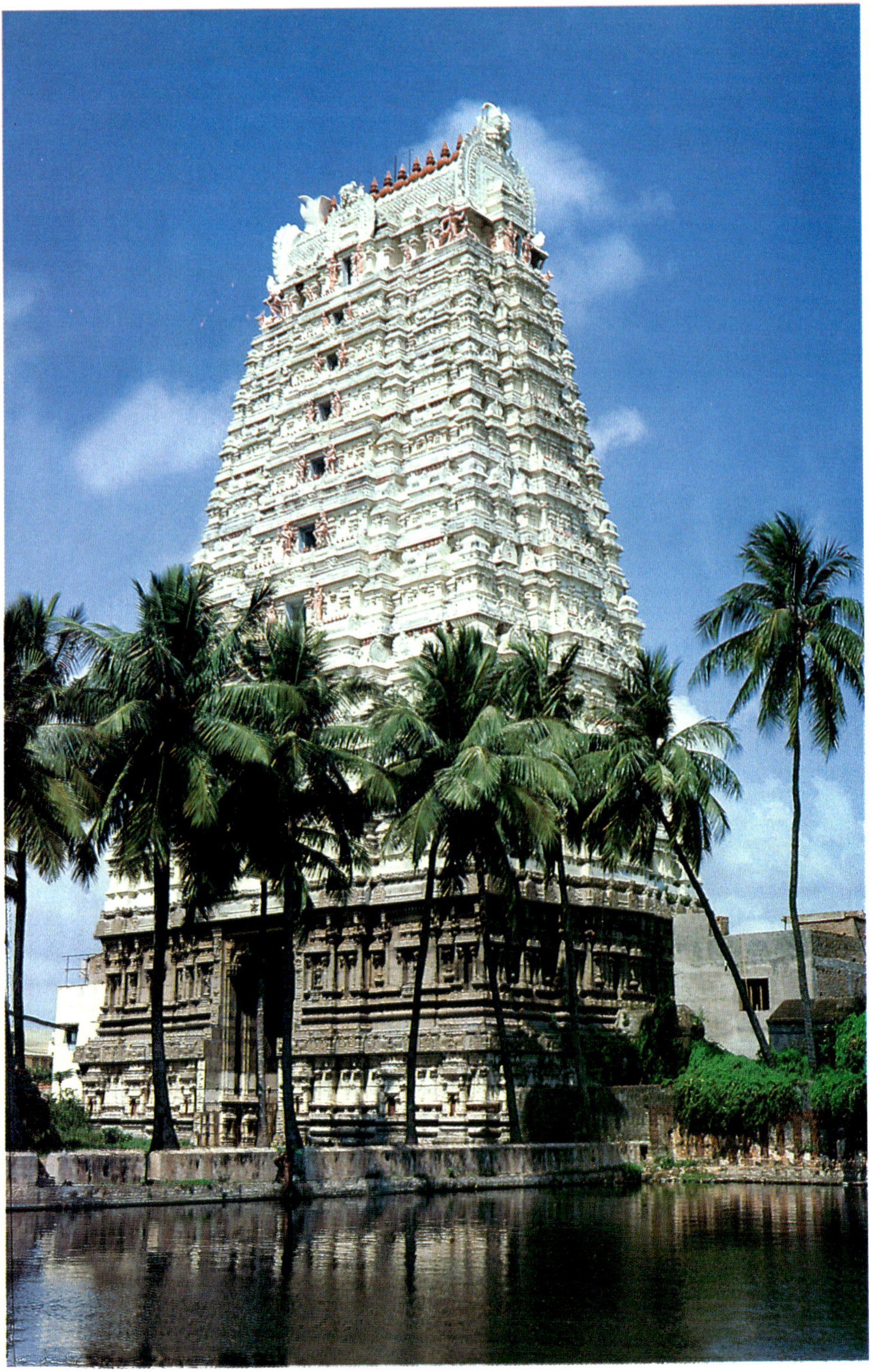

Fig. 26 North Gōpura and Nandi Tīrtham

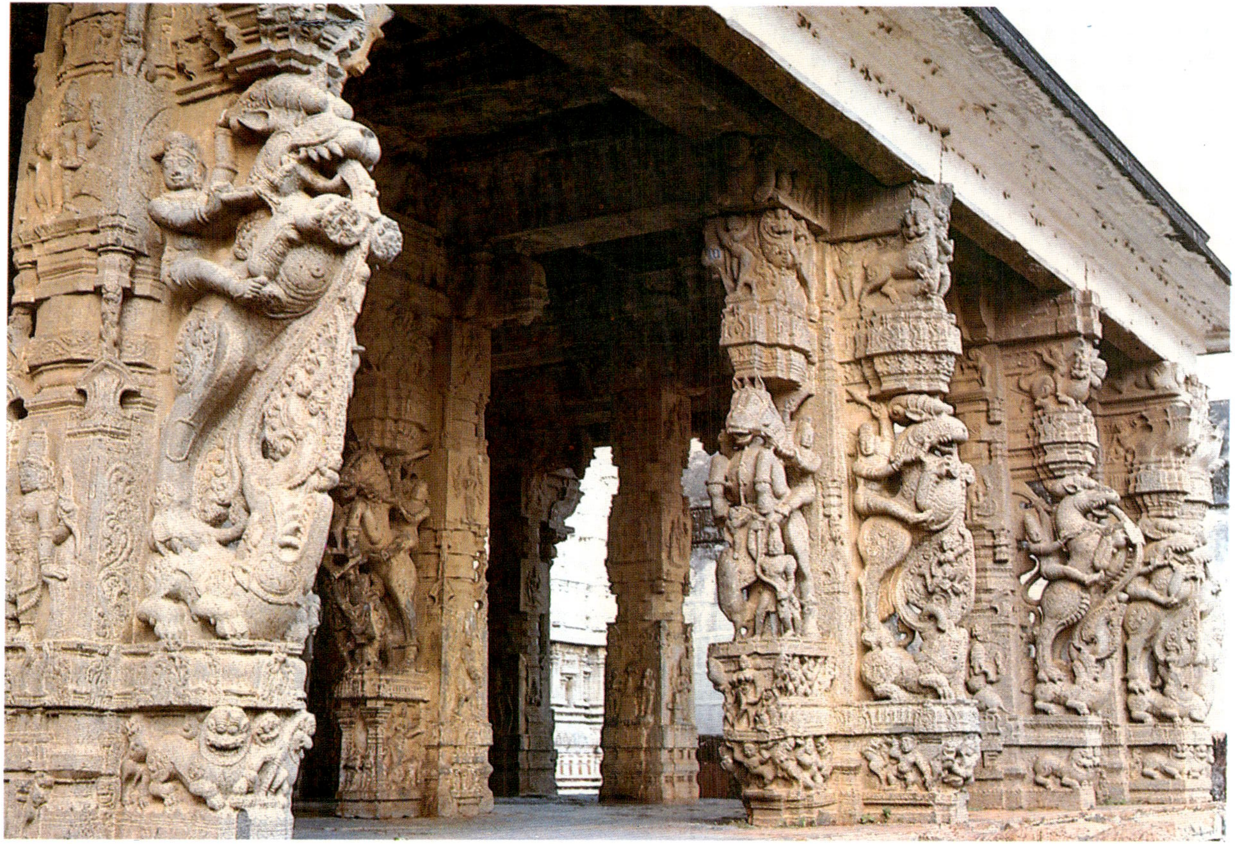

Fig. 27 Āmai Mandapa

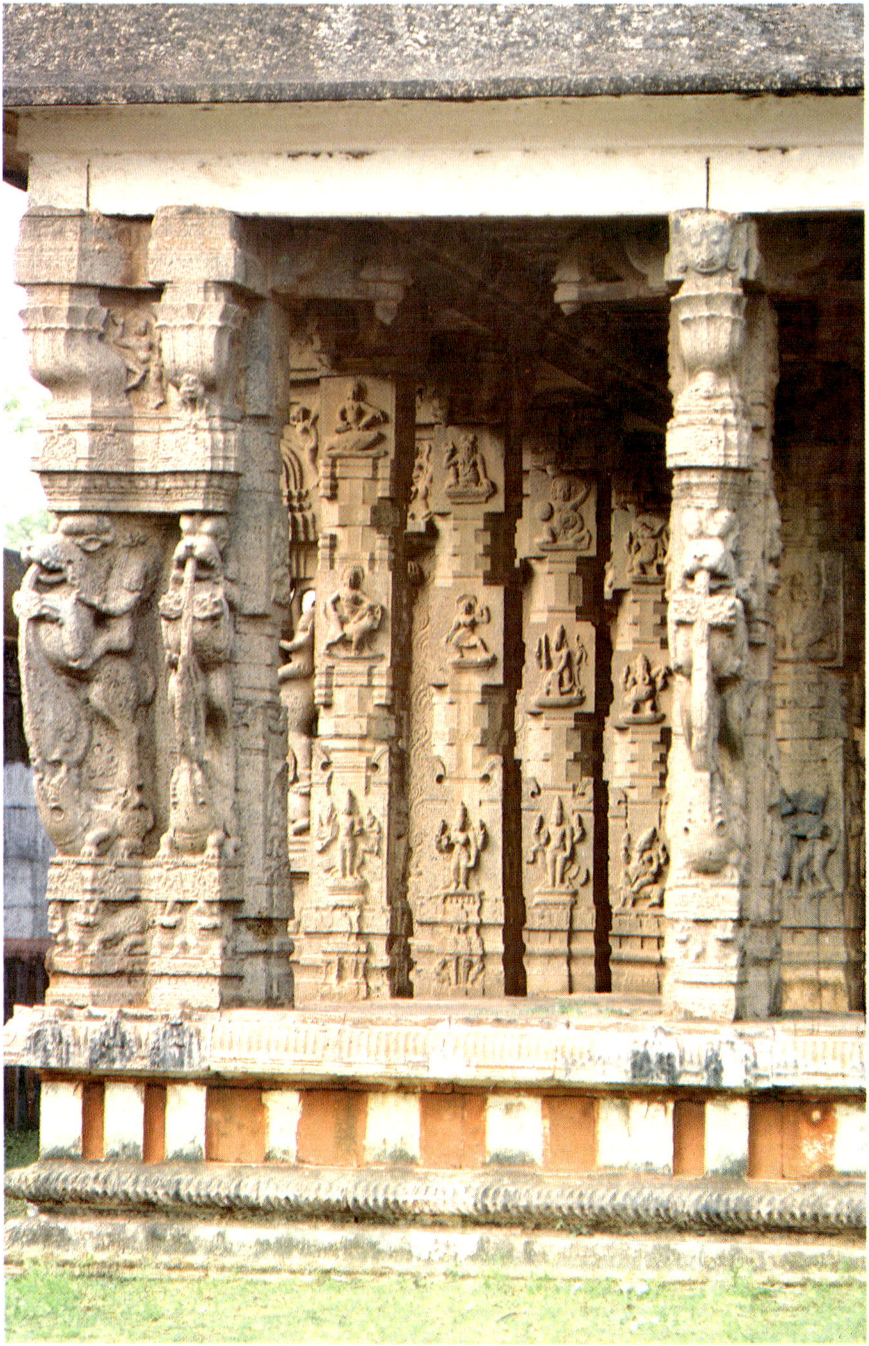

Fig. 28 Āmai Mandapa

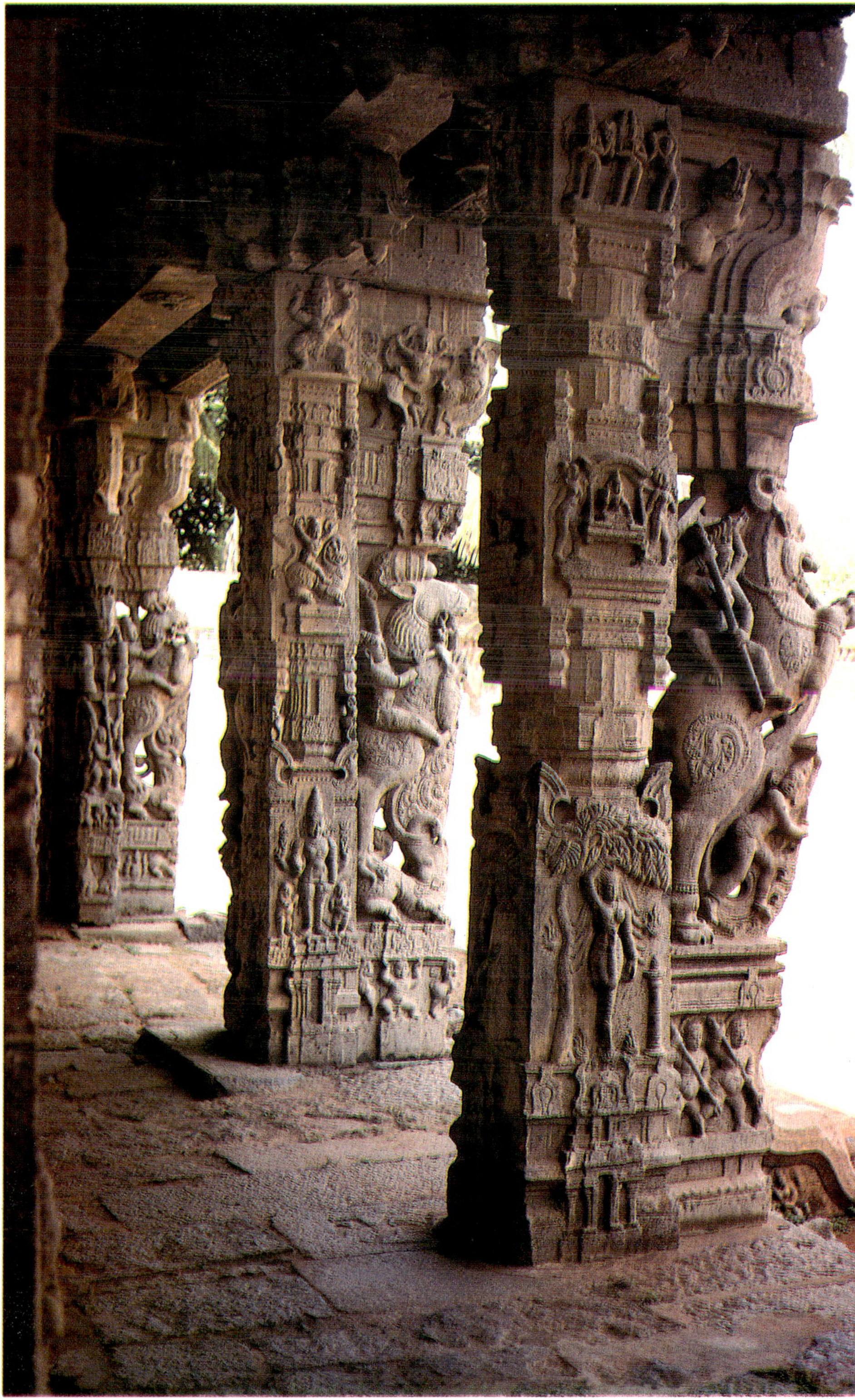

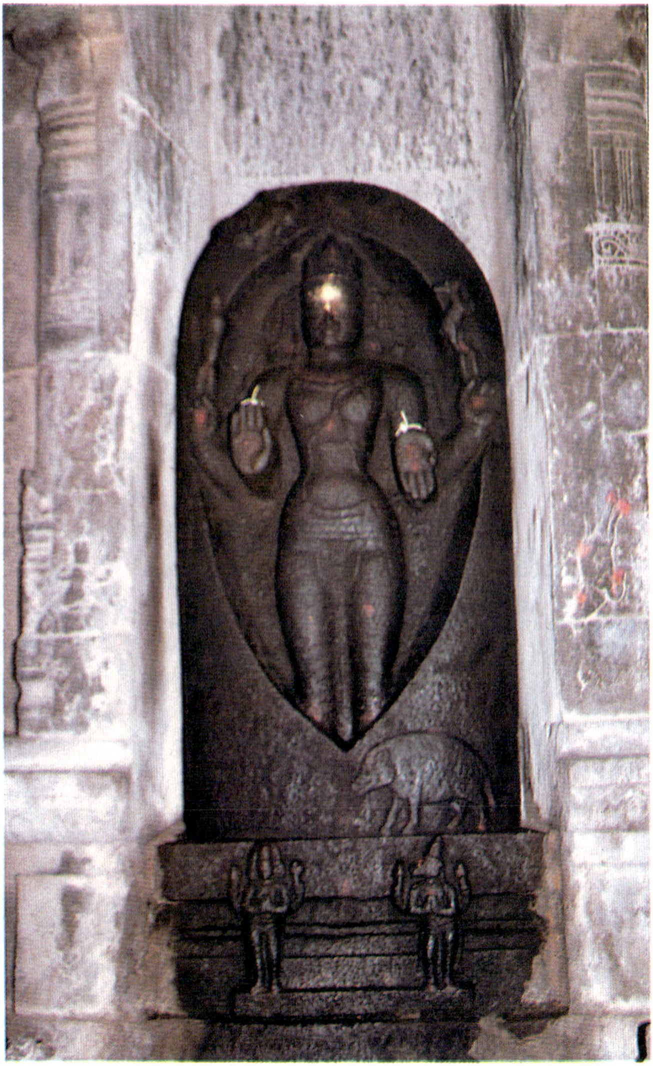

Fig. 30 Lingodbhava Bhaktavatsala Temple

←Fig. 29 Āmai Mandapa

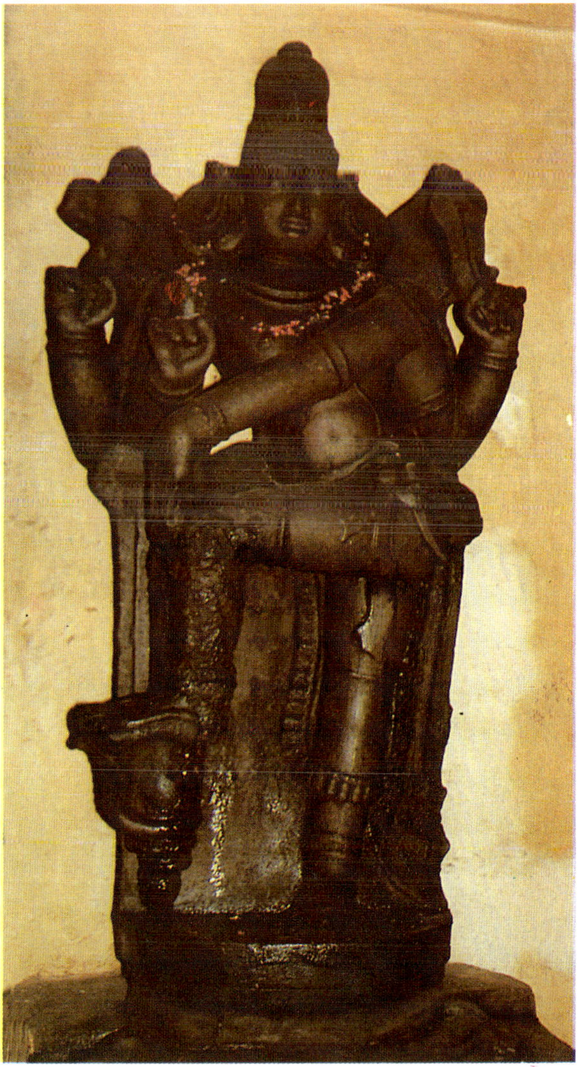

Fig. 31 Dvārapālaka, Bhaktavatsala Temple

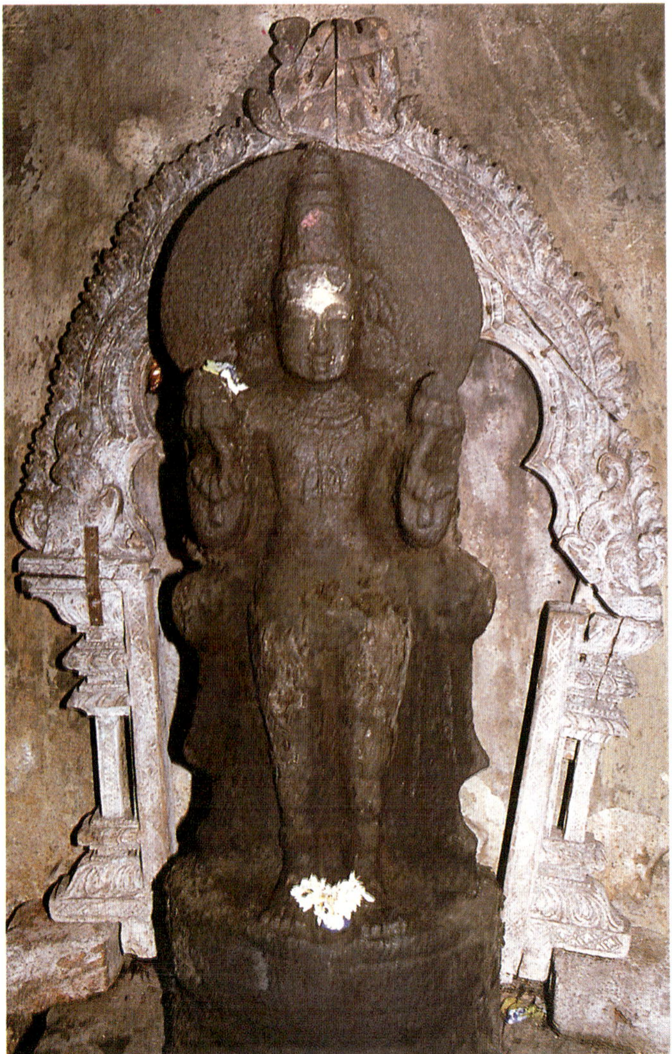

Fig. 32 Sūrya, Bhaktavatsala Temple

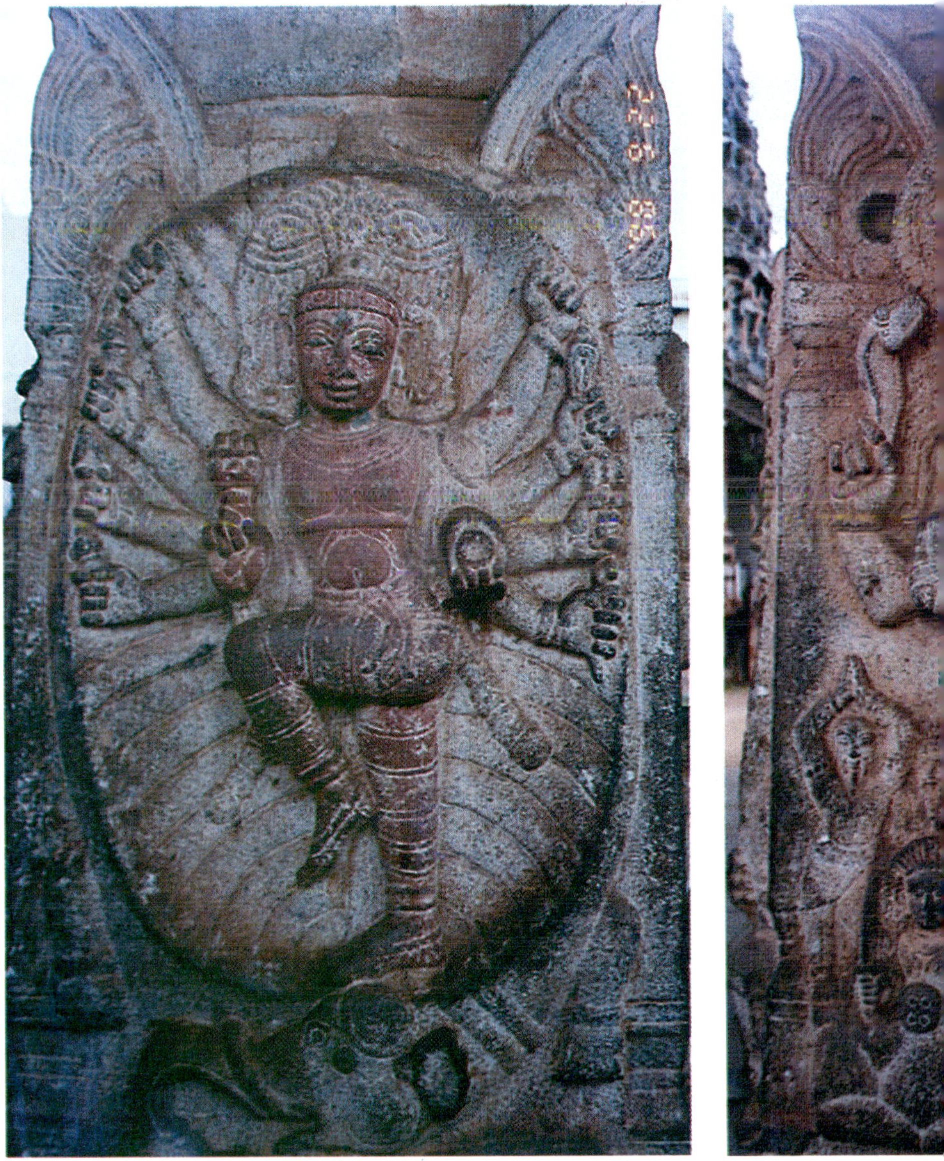

Fig. 33 Gajasamhāra Mūrti

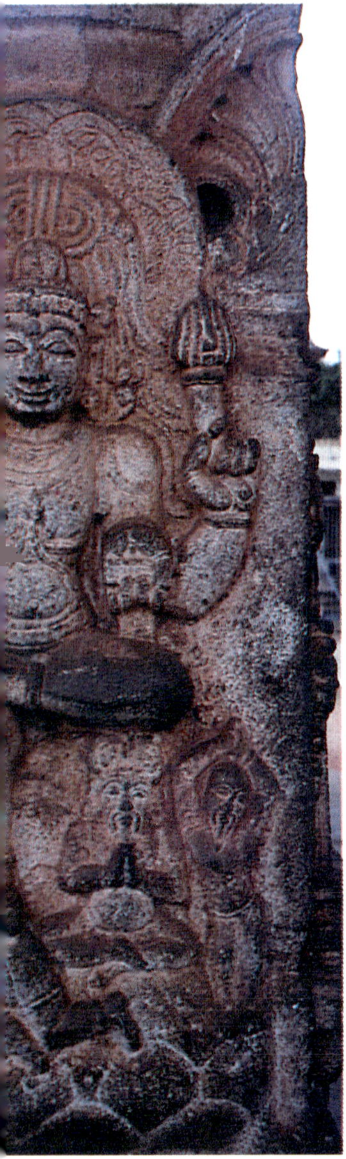

Fig. 34 Dakṣiṇāmūrti

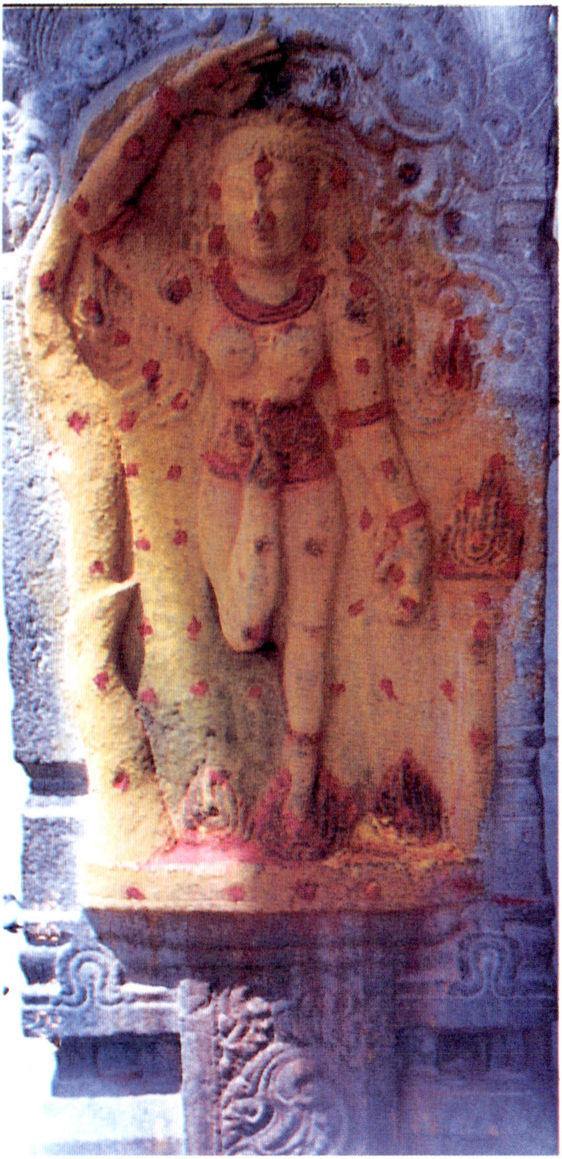

Fig. 35 Pārvatī in penance

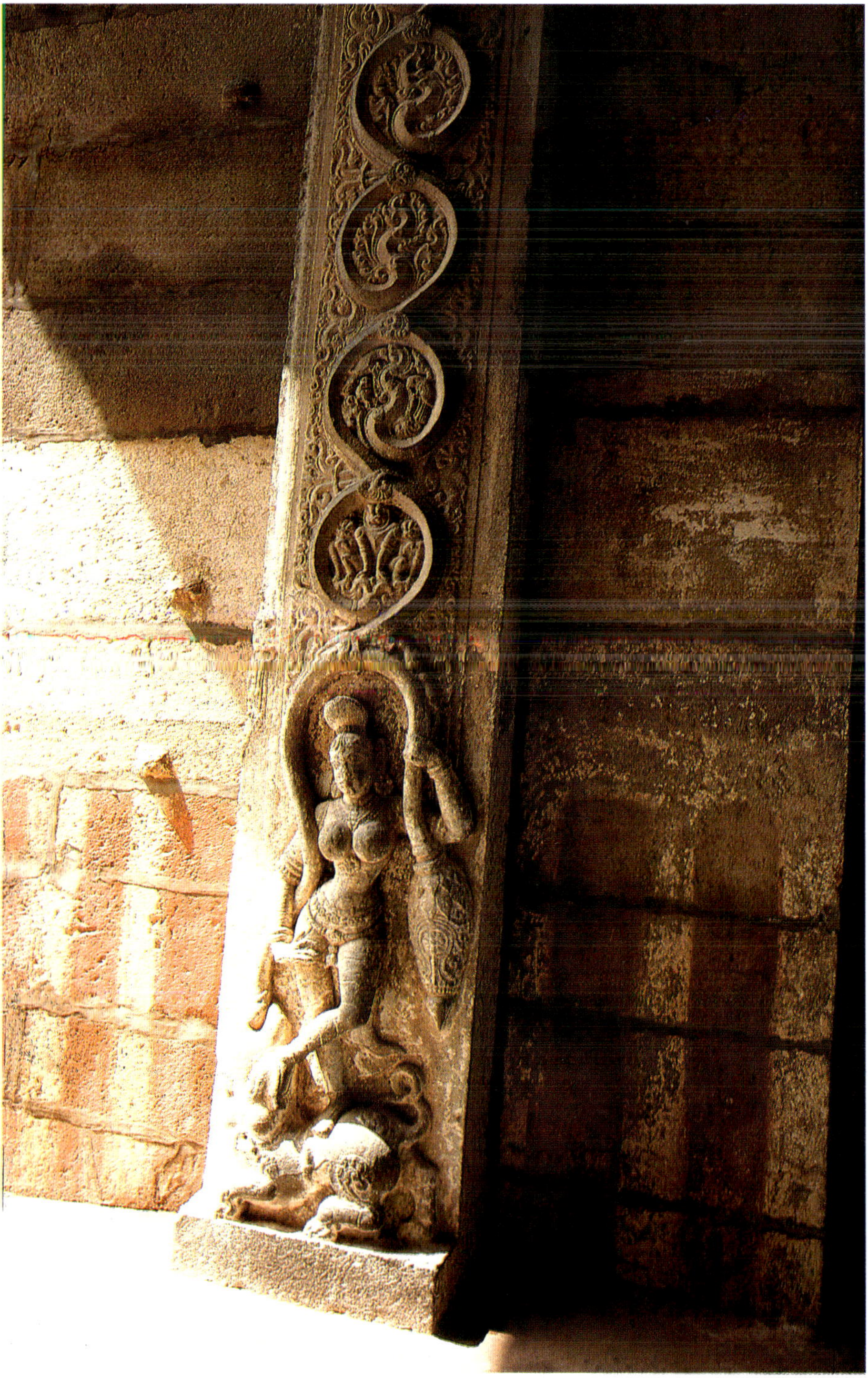

Fig. 36 River Goddess Gaṅga

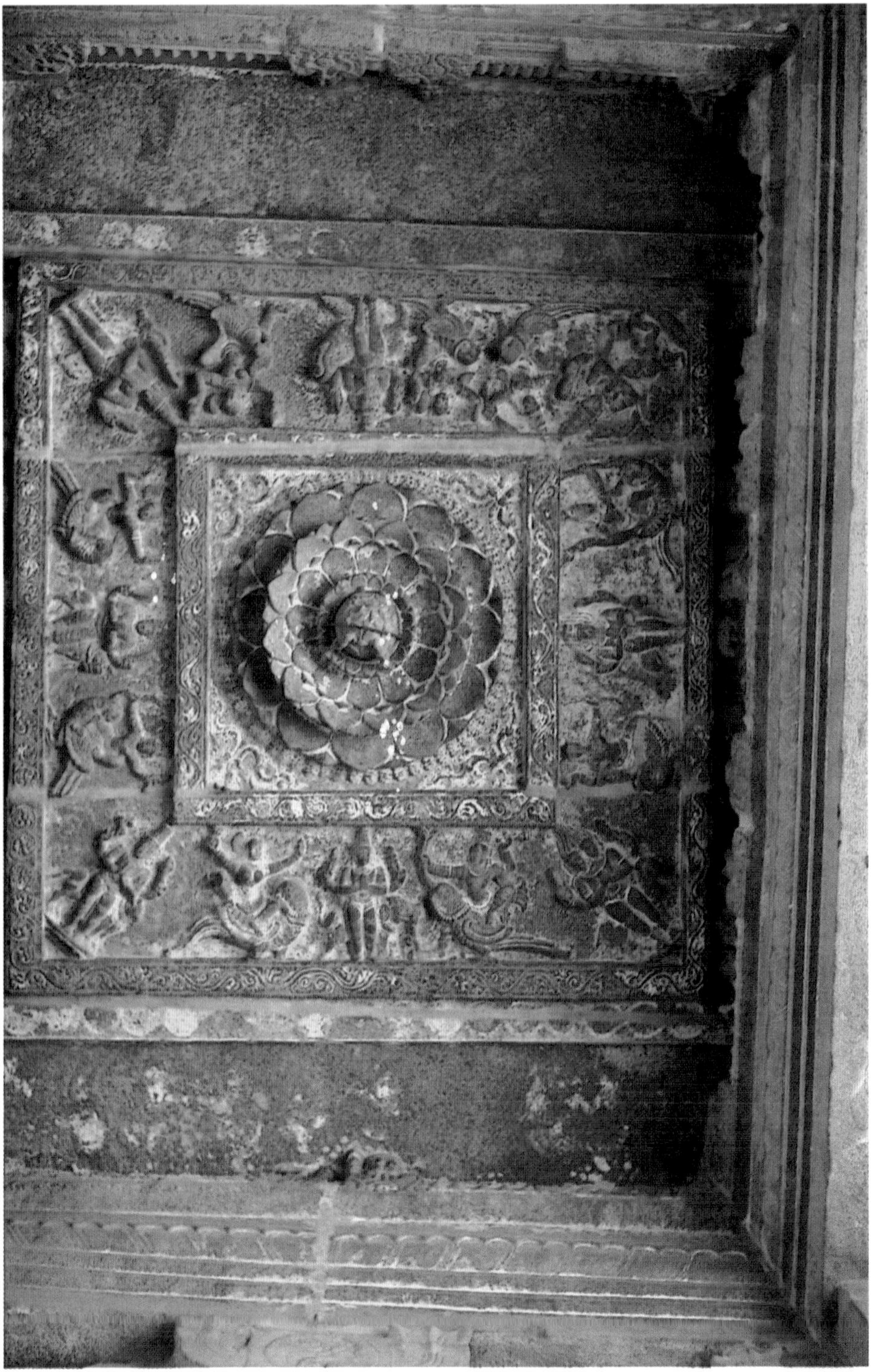

Fig. 38 Western Gōpura ceiling

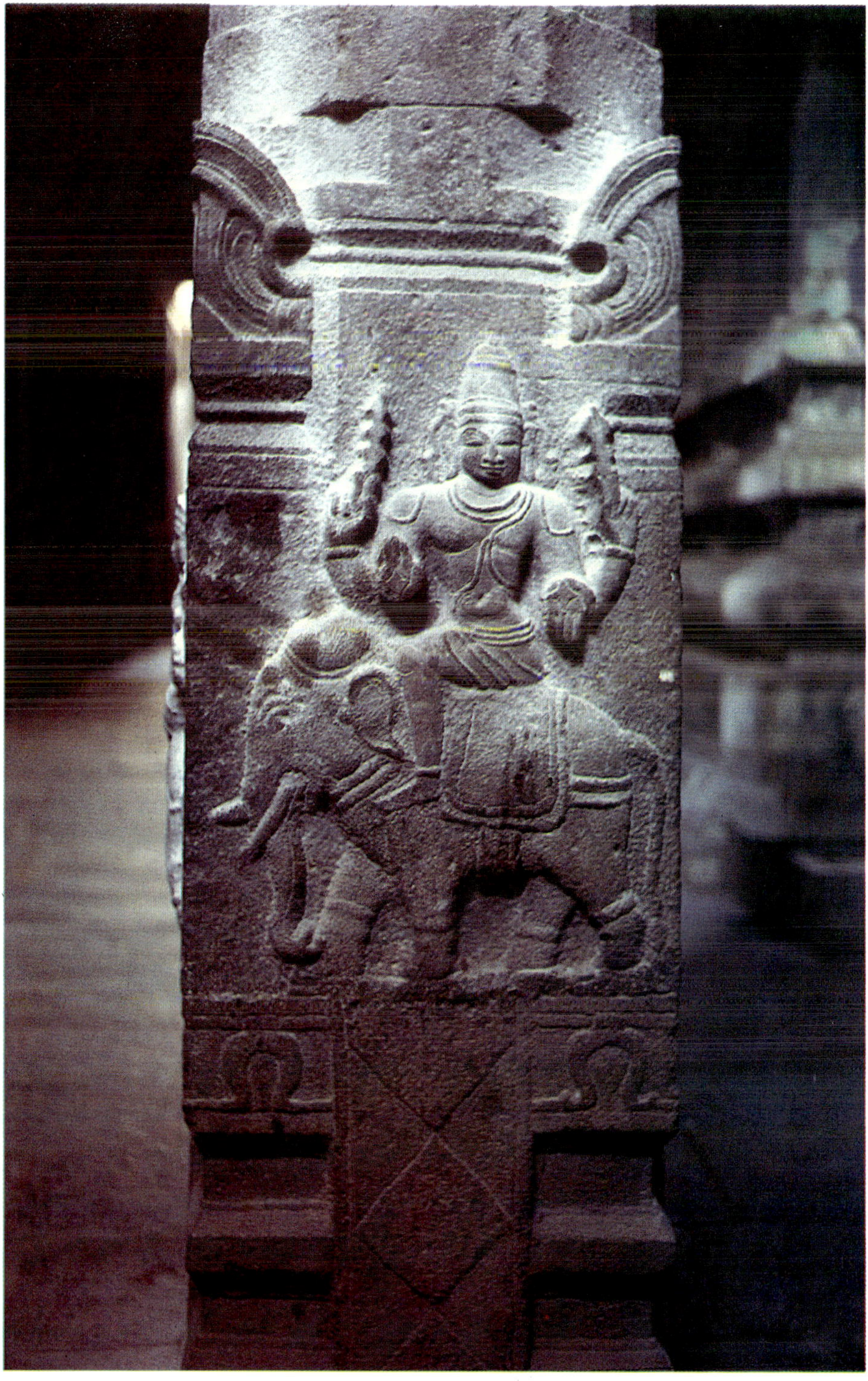

Fig. 39 Indra

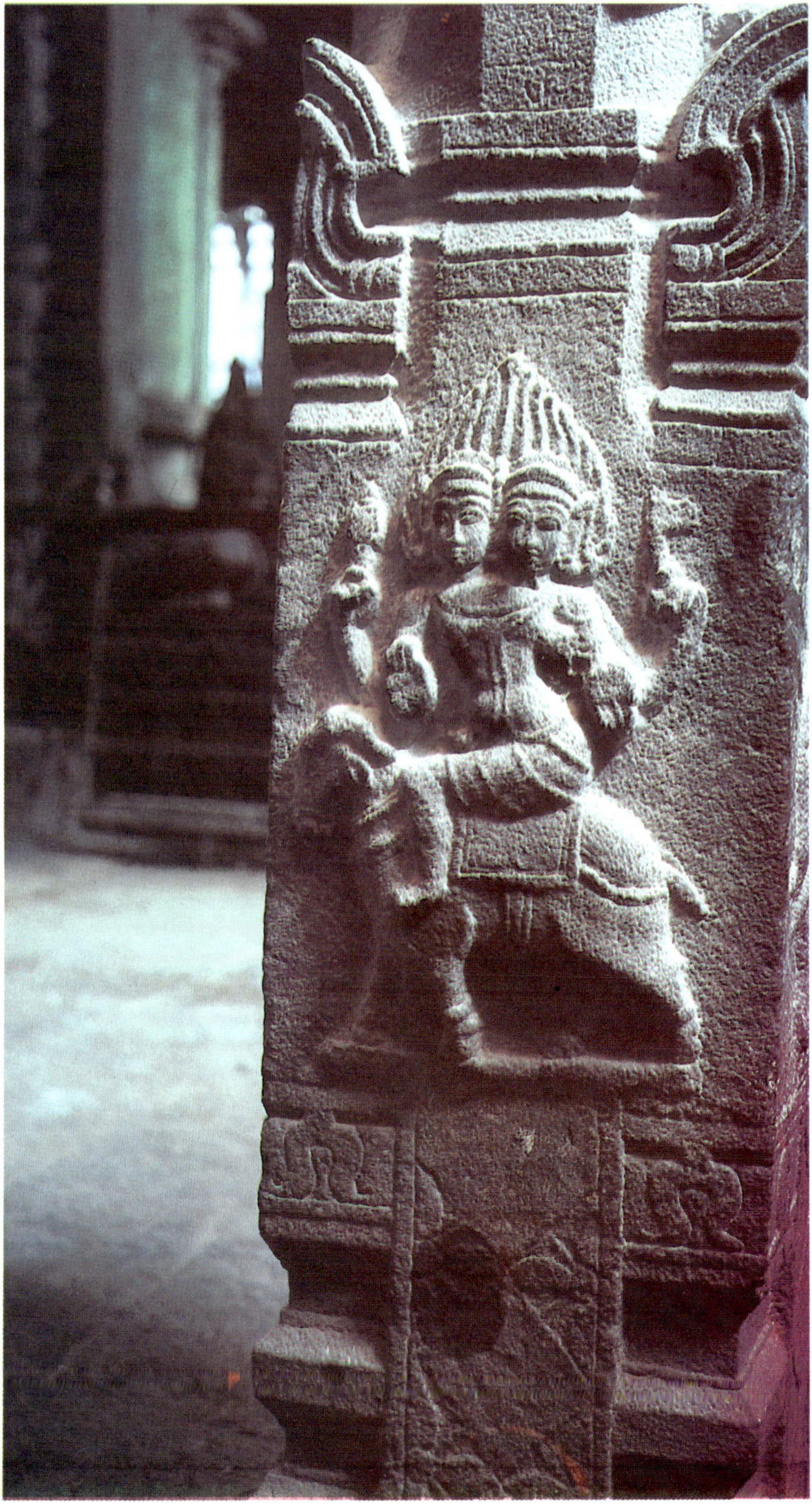

Fig. 40 Agni

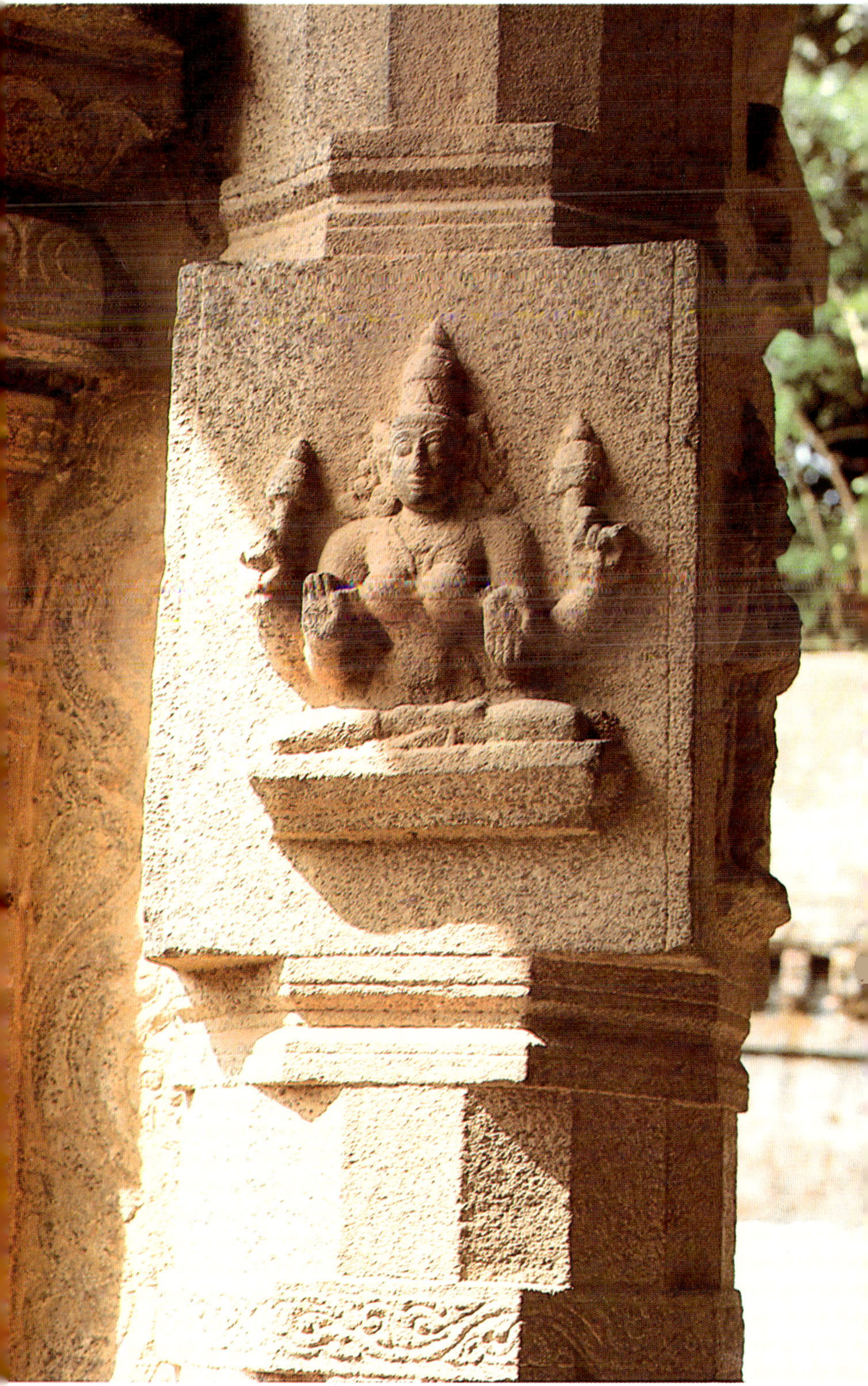

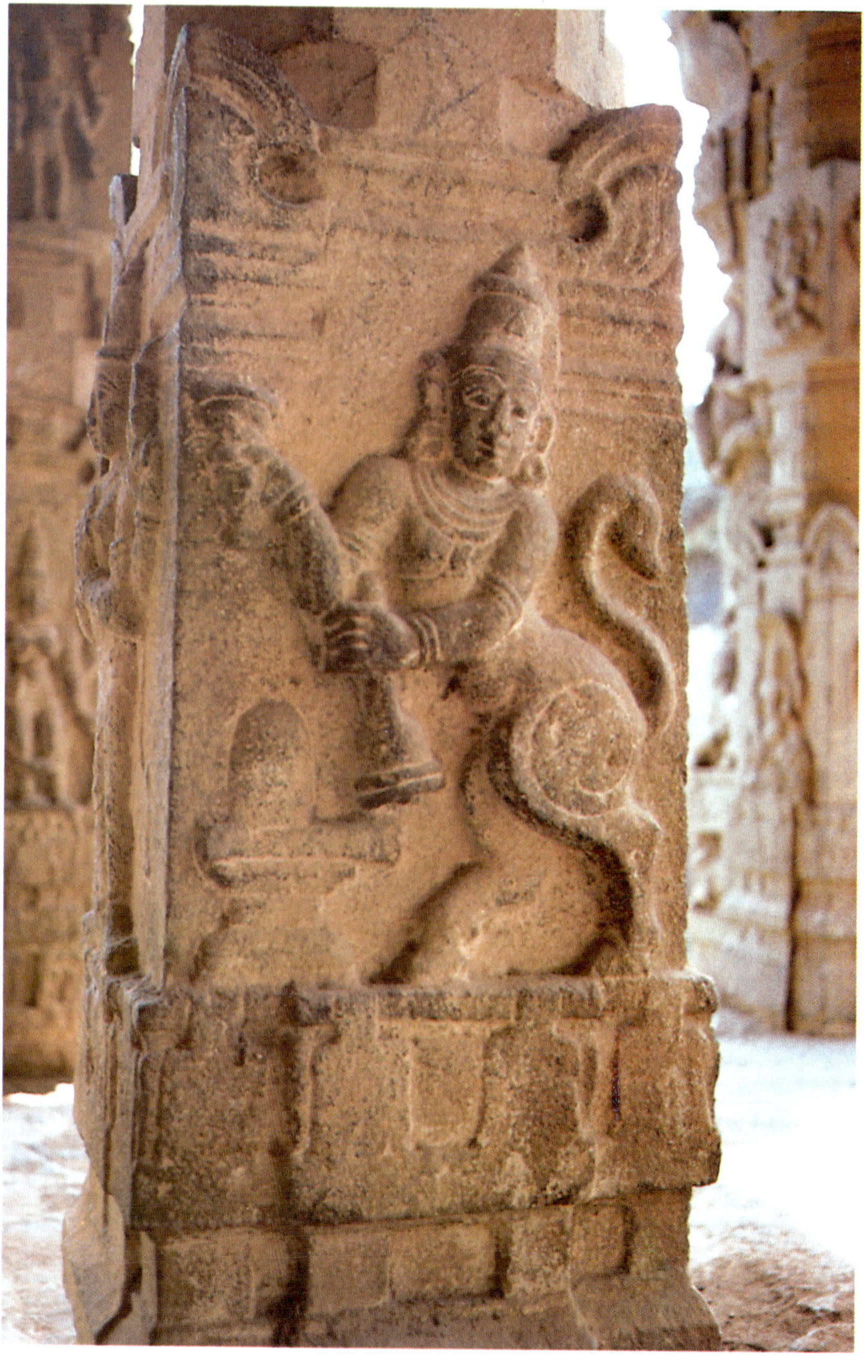

Fig. 42 Vyāgrapāda

←Fig. 41 Lakṣmī

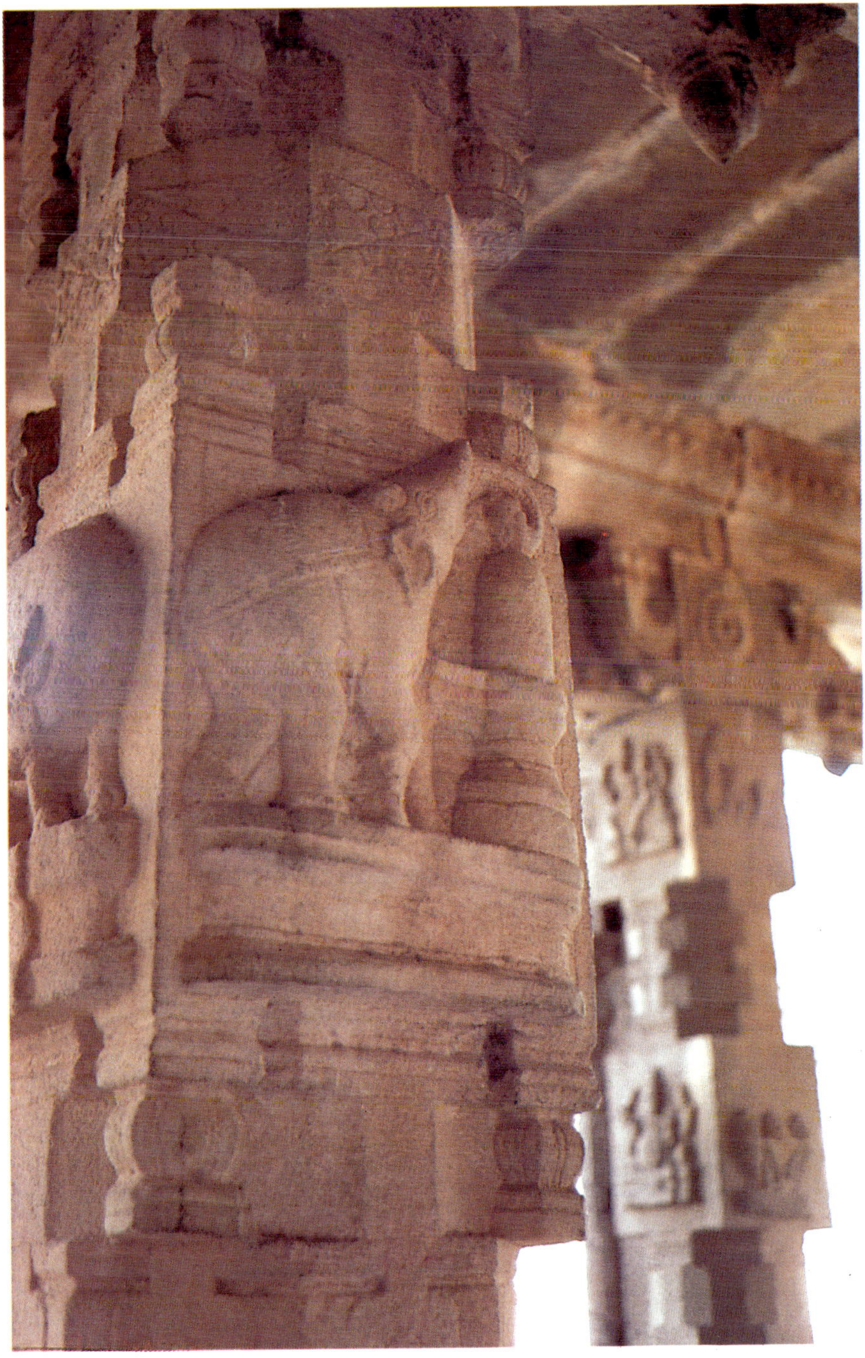

Fig. 43 Elephant worshipping Linga

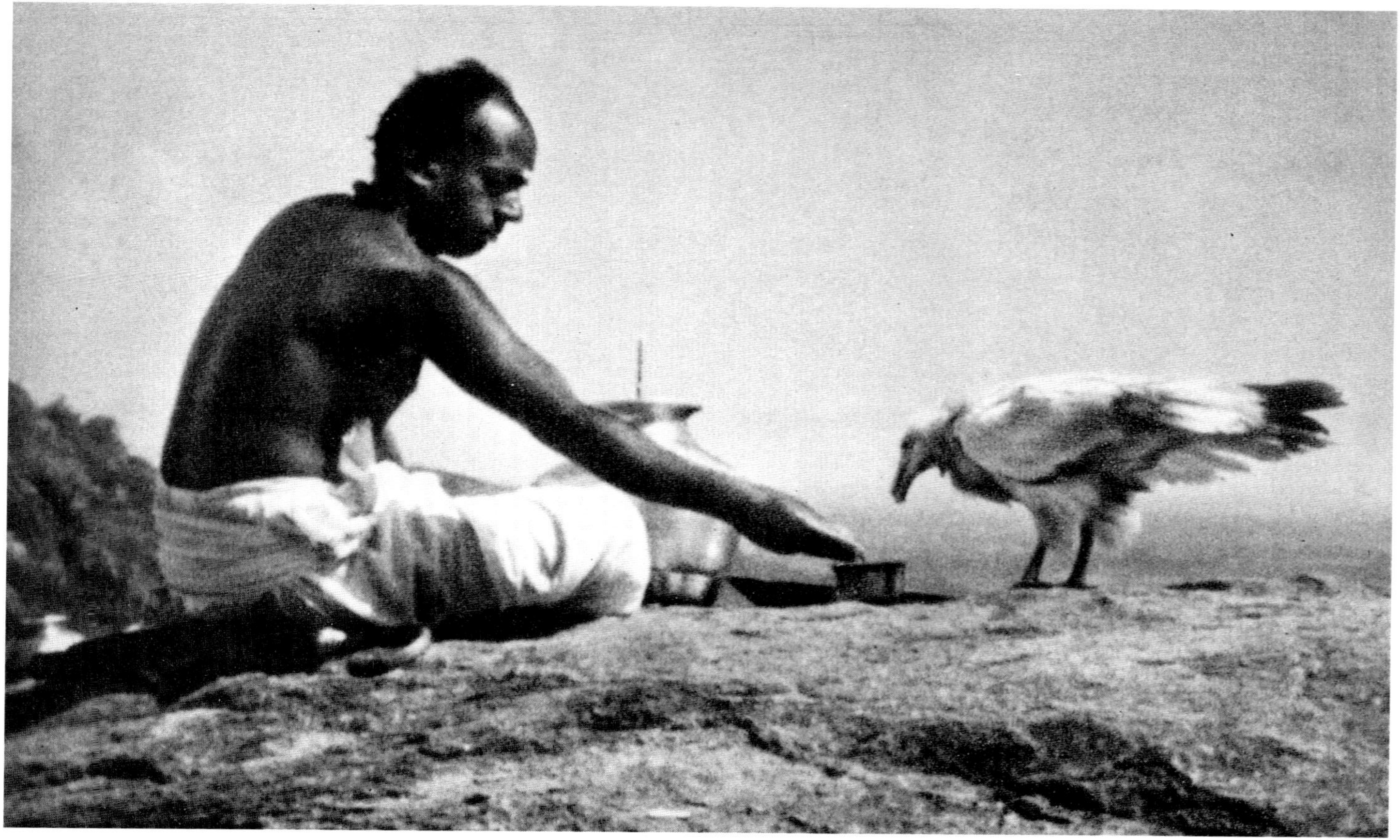

Fig. 6 Priest feeding the eagles

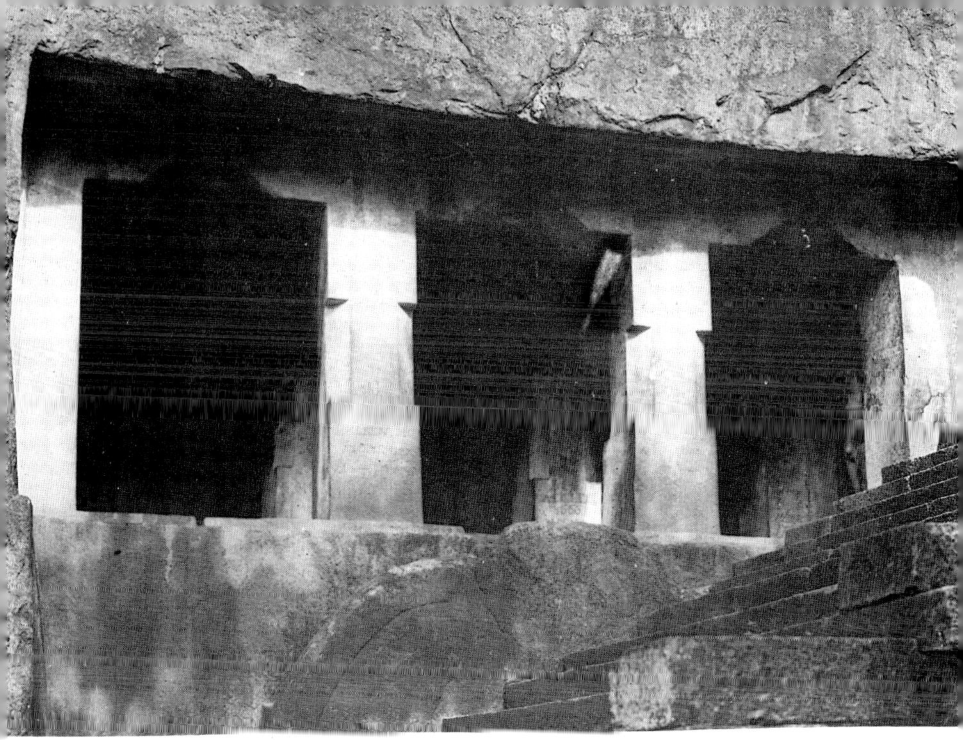

Fig. 3 Orukal Mandapa

Fig. 7 Dvārapālakas in the Orukal Mandapa

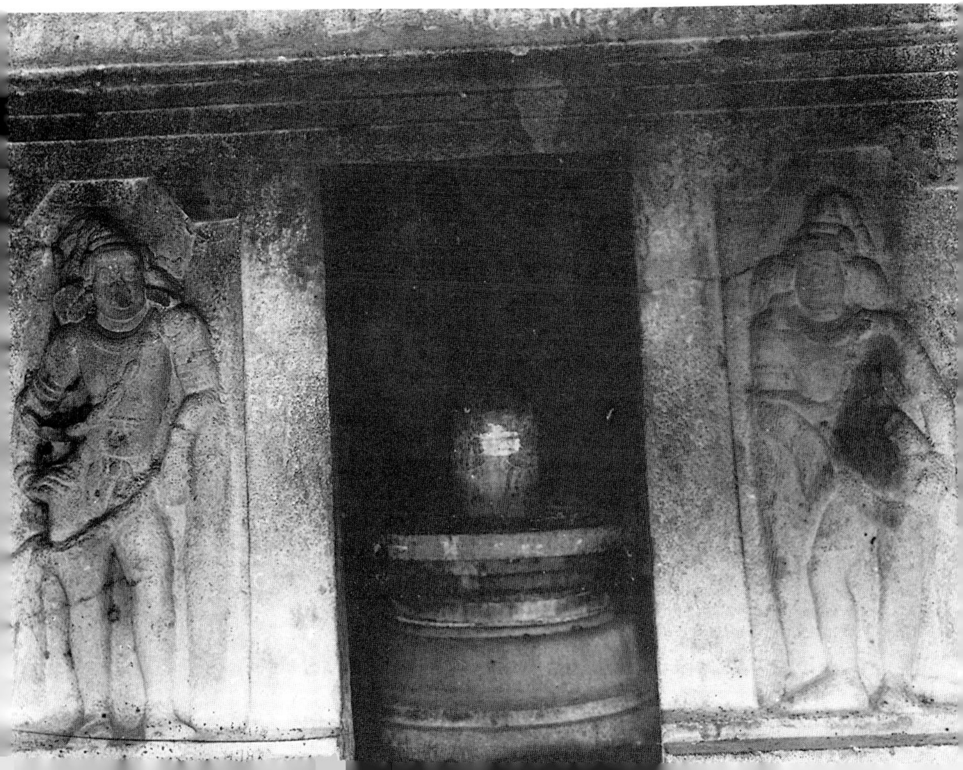

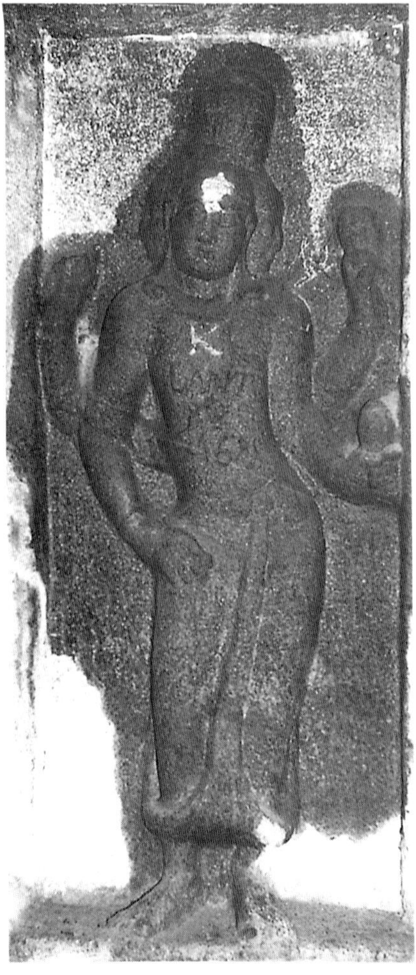

Fig. 8 Brahmā

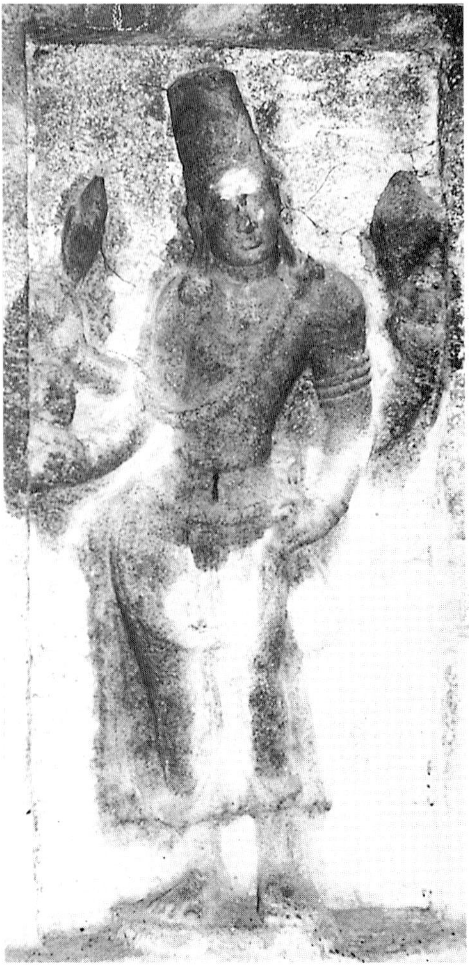

Fig. 9 Viṣṇu

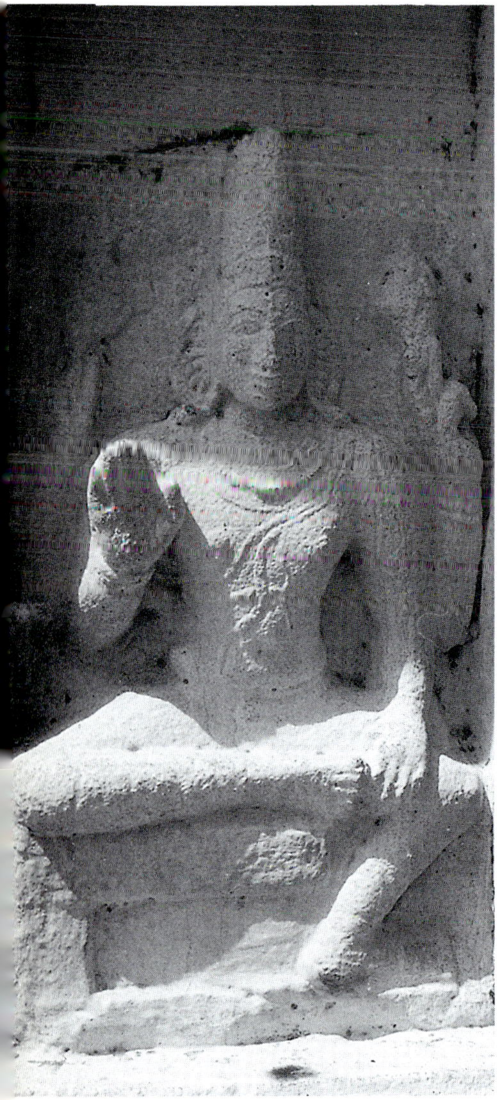

Fig. 14 Viṣṇu (northern niche)

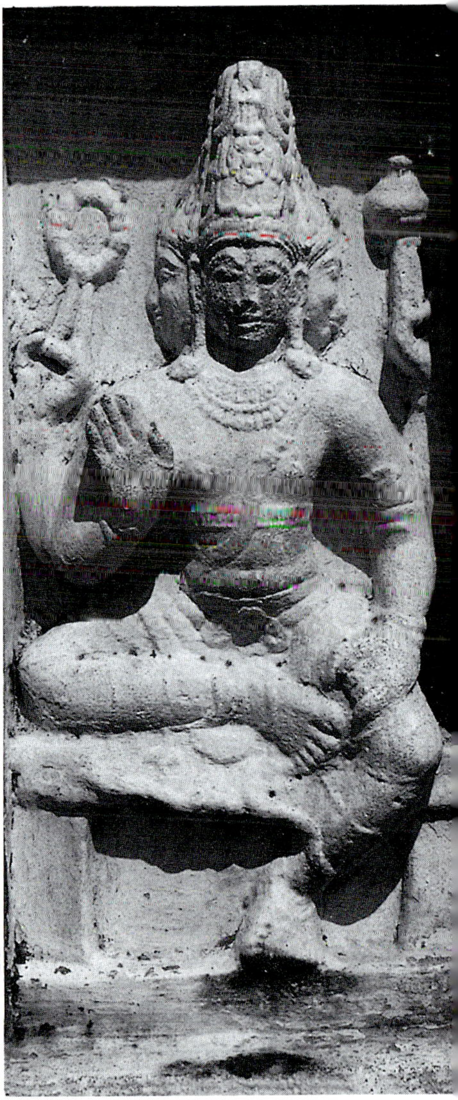

Fig. 15 Brahmā

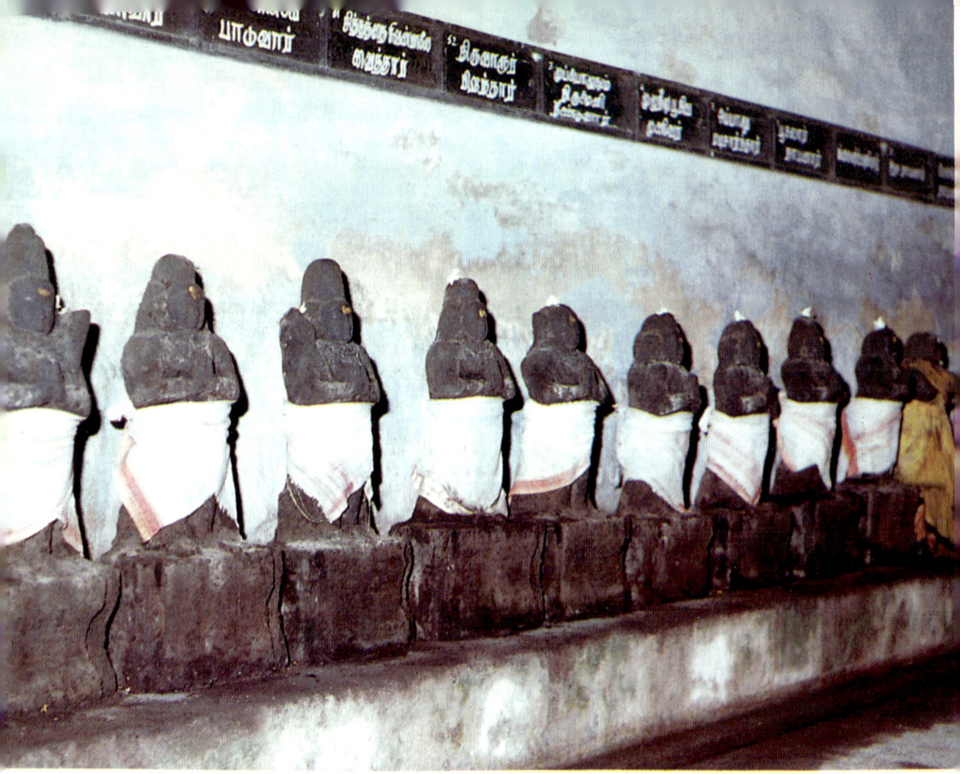

Fig. 37 Śaiva Saints (Nāyanmārs)

Fig. 46 Śaiva Saints (South Gōpura entrance)

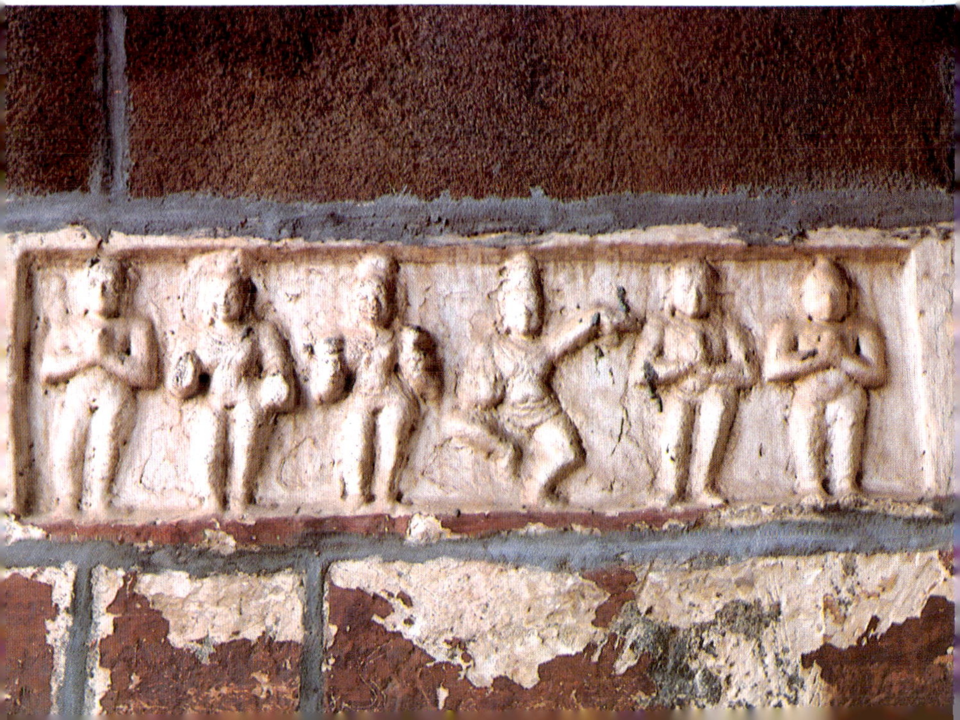

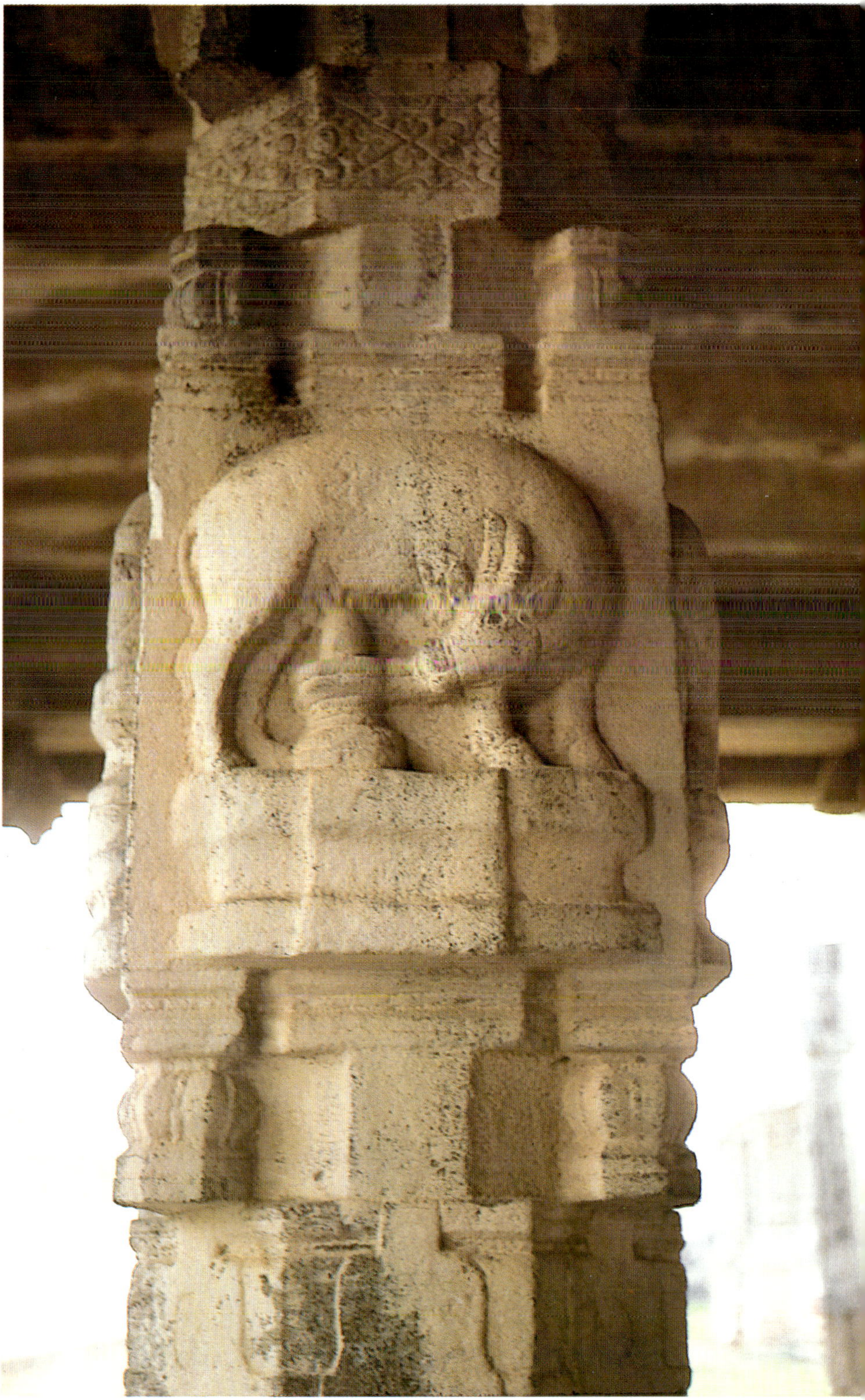

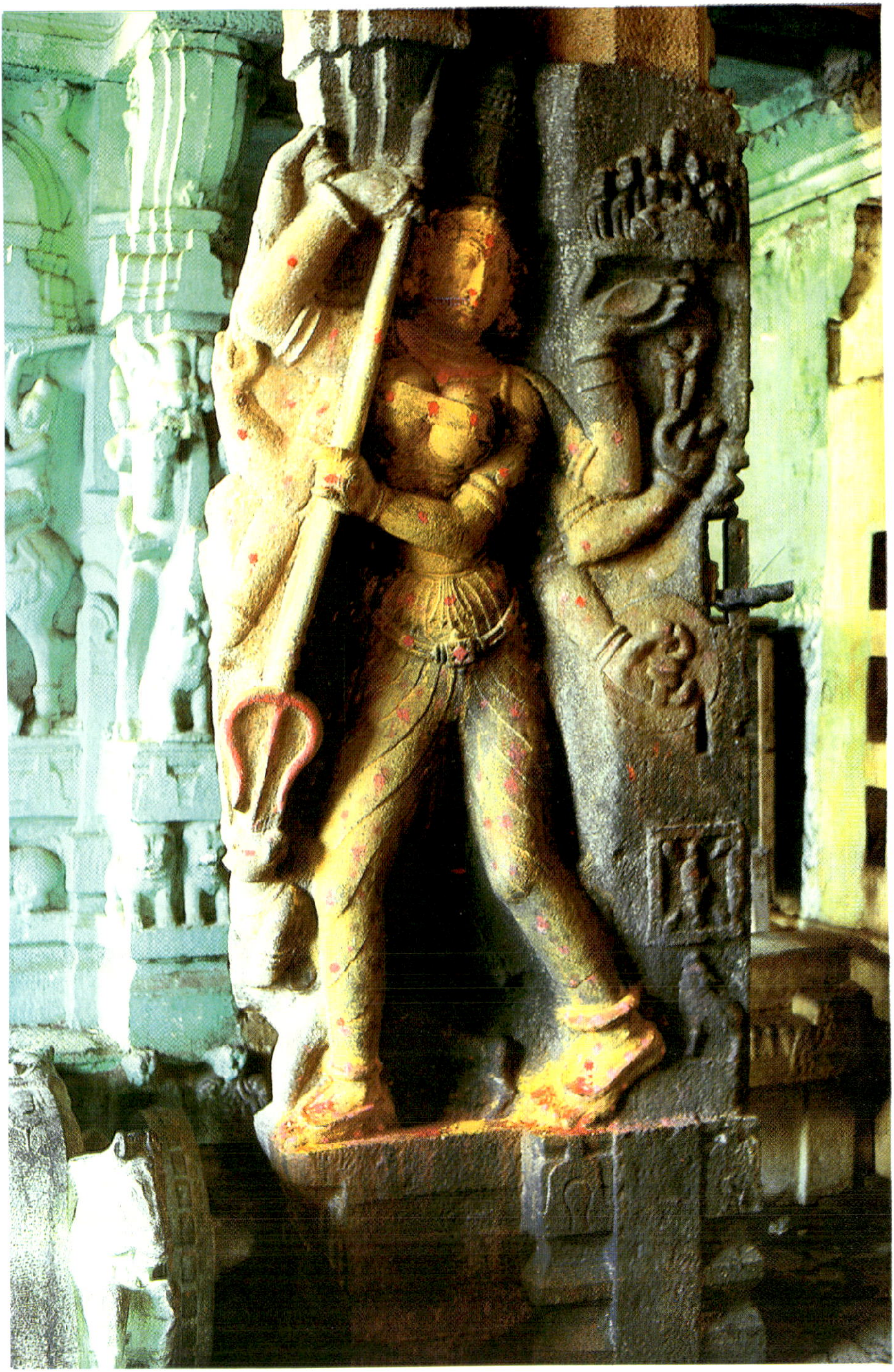

Fig. 45 Durga

← Fig. 44 Cow pouring its milk over the Linga

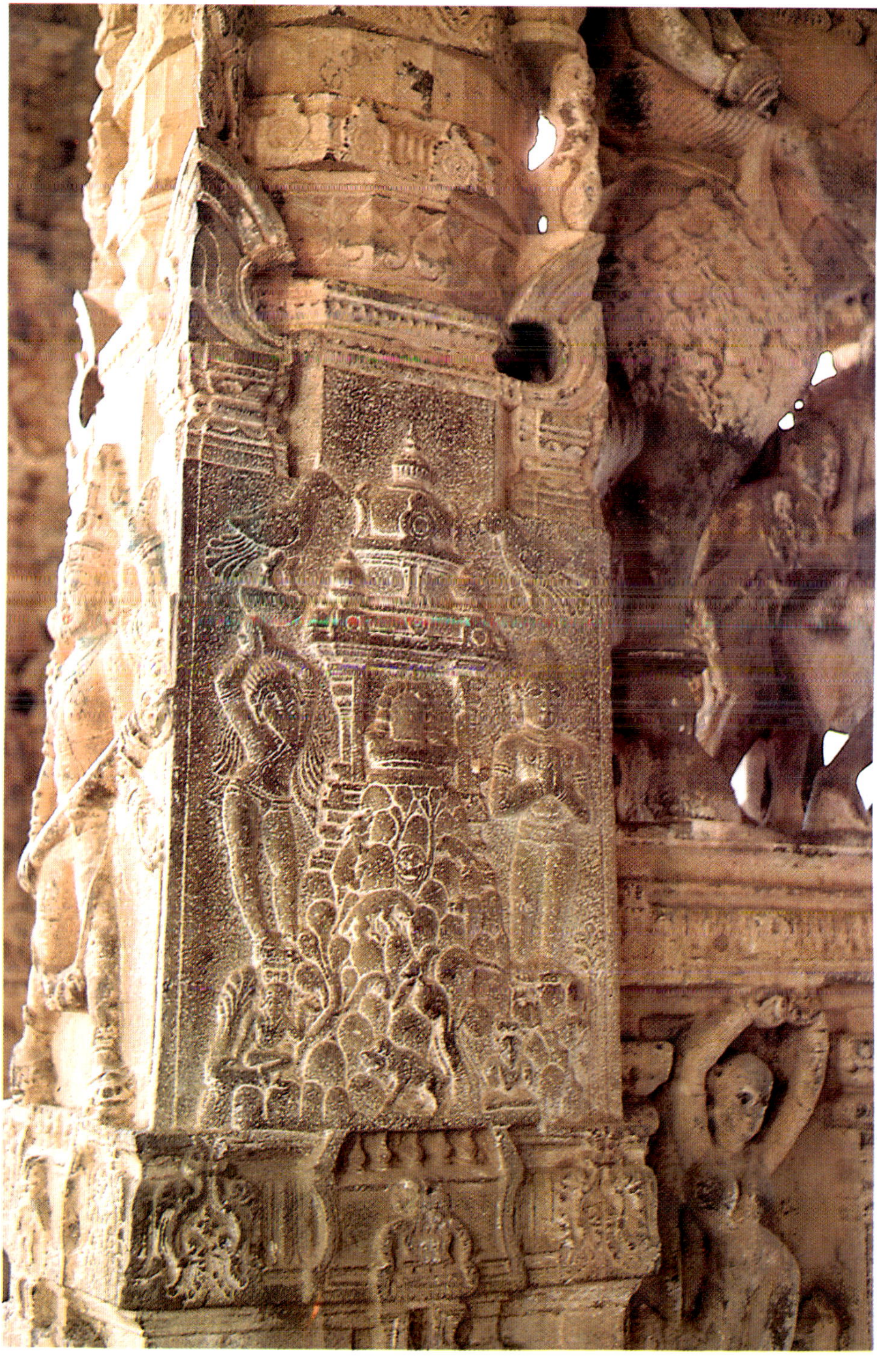

Fig. 47 Hill Temple with two eagles

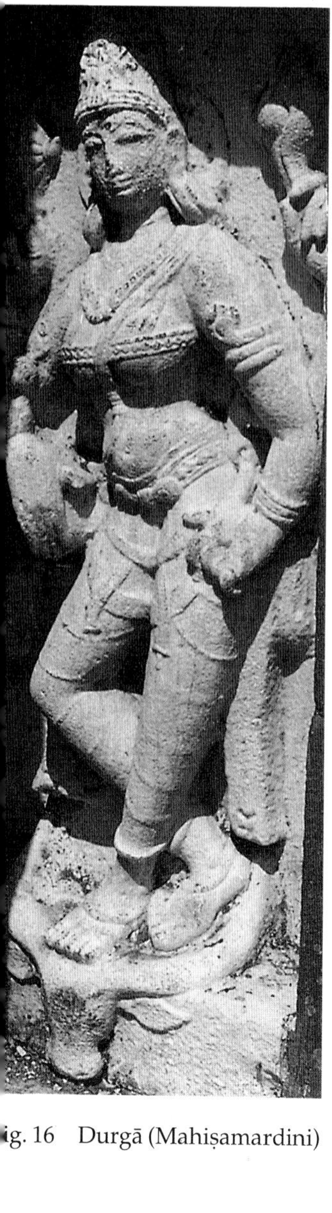

ig. 16 Durgā (Mahiṣamardini)

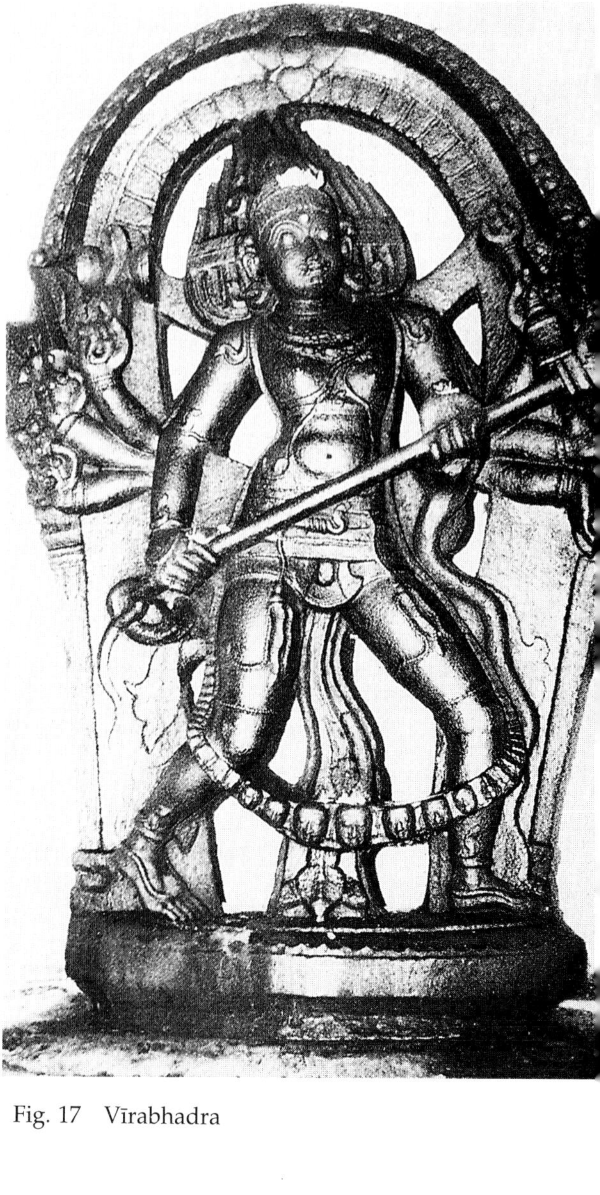

Fig. 17 Vīrabhadra

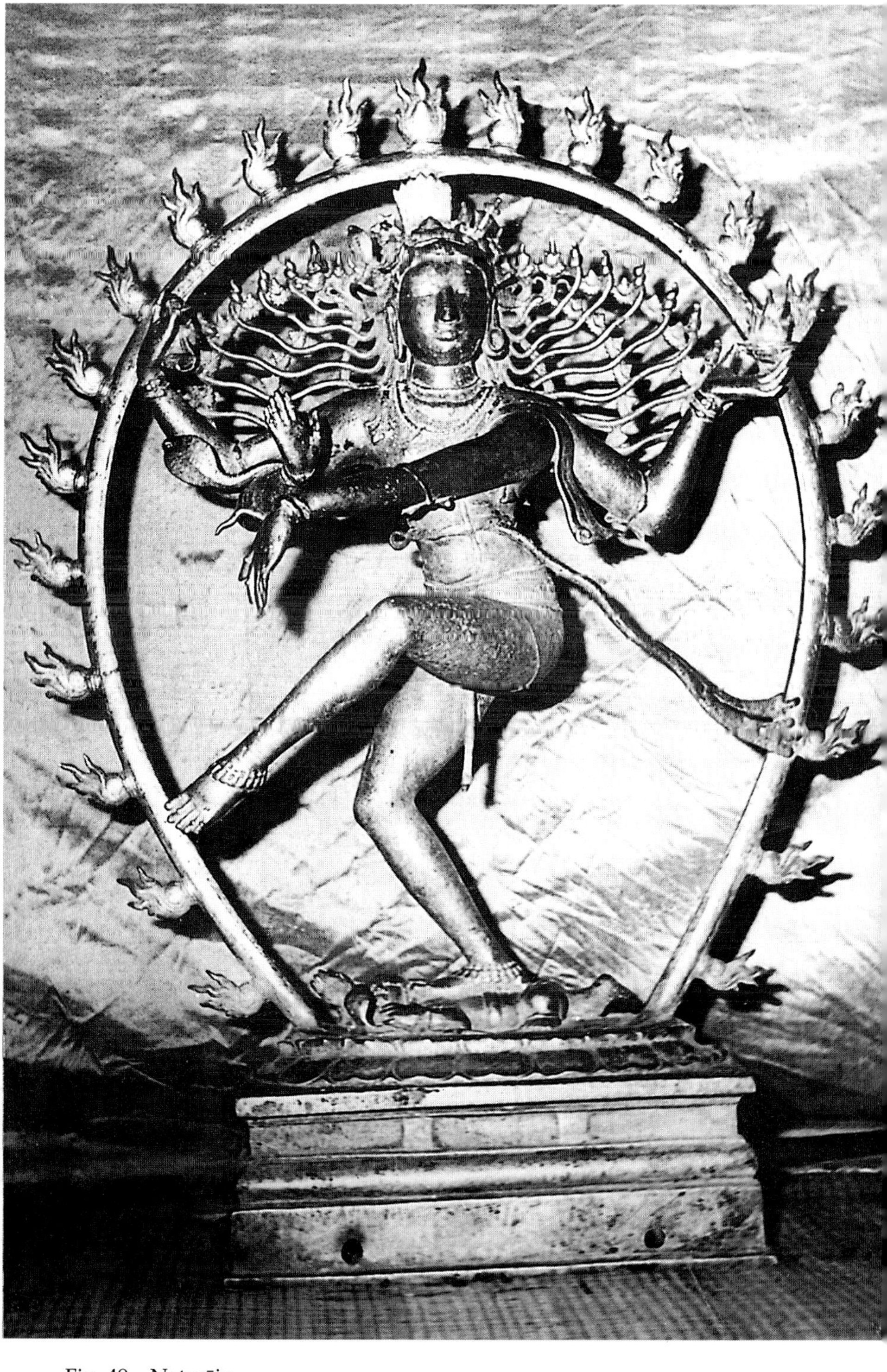

Fig. 49 Naṭarāja

from the coast westward to the foot of the hill which forms part of the Eastern Ghats. The land is flat and dreary near the sea, undulating and hilly in the west.

Tirukkaḷukkuṉṟam and its environs present undulating plains, varied by ridged or conical hills which rarely attain a height exceeding 600 ft. On the main hill at the place, called Vedagiri, 500 ft. in height, stands the temple of Lord Vedagirīś-vara (Figs. 1 and 2). Half-way up the hill is the Orukal Mandapa, a rock-cut temple of Māmalla of 7th century (Fig. 3). Down the hill, there is a large temple with four gateways or gopuras dedicated to Lord Bhaktavatsala and his consort, Tirupurasundari (Fig. 4). There are three holy tanks, Pakṣi-tīrtham on the hill, Sanku-tīrtham down the hill and Nandi-tīrtham inside the Bhaktavatsala temple (Fig. 5).

CLIMATE

The climate of the place is temperate. On account of its proximity to the sea, it is fairly humid. The place is affected by both the monsoons. From the middle of October till the beginning of February, the North-East wind blows over the region. The wind then becomes South-East or South till the middle of May. Thereupon, though the hot land-winds set in, they are tempered by the sea-breeze generally beginning soon after midday and continuing until late in the night.

The proximity to the sea is not however an unmixed blessing. The place, like the Chingleput district as a whole, is peculiarly liable to visitation of cyclones. The most frequent period for the occurrence of such cyclones is during October and November. They are generated in the Bay of Bengal and mostly confined to the coast between hundred miles north and hundred miles south of Madras. These cyclones which are often periodical caused much destruction in the past.

GEOLOGY

The soil of the Chingleput taluk is mostly red ferrunginous loam in the interior, and sand towards the east. Being covered with low hills and extensive shrub jungles, the soil is generally rocky and therefore poor. But a small proportion of the area is free from such drawbacks and Tirukkaḷukkuṉṟam and its immediate surroundings are fairly fertile, particularly in the recent past when bore wells and electric pumps have enabled large area of lands to be brought under cultivation.

The rocks of the area are mainly of the granite variety. This is hardly the ideal material for architectural or sculptural activity. Yet, as it was the easily and readily available raw material, the artisans of the area have exploited it to the best of their ability and Māmallapuram and Tirukkaḷukkuṉṟam stand today as testimony to the height they could rise in the spheres in spite of the hard raw material on hand. To what greater heights they would have risen had they been given a soft stone like sandstone, may easily be imagined.

VEGETATION

The vast expanse of the paddy fields in the neighbourhood of the hill, Vedagiri, presents a pleasant sight to see. Rice cultivation is the main crop though not the only one. Sugarcane, groundnuts, Bengalgram, and ragi are also cultivated. There are also the useful palmyra, tamarind and mango trees.

The range of hills near Tirukkaḷukkuṉṟam are said to contain medicinal herbs. There has been, through the ages, a firm belief that on account of the effect of the variety of medicinal herbs growing on the hill, a *pradakṣiṇā* or going round the sacred hill of Vedagiri cures one of diseases. Indeed, it is a common sight even to this day to see people going round the hill in the morning and evening. This is a unique feature of the place. The place is recommended to the sick people as a good health-resort.

SCENERY AND THE LAYOUT OF THE VILLAGE

The top of the hill, Vedagiri, commands an enchanting view of the landscape. On the south lies the famous Sankutīrtham (conch) tank with a *maṇḍapa* at the centre. On the west is the temple of Bhaktavatsalēśvara and Tirupurasundari, with a number of the principal streets on four sides of the temple which add to the charm of the scenery. The temple was the nucleus round which the village has grown. The streets are regularly formed, the houses are built close to each other. To the east of the hill, Vedagiri, is the Mūvarpēṭṭai, so called because of the sacred visit of the Śaiva trio, Appar, Sambandar and Sundarar, who visited the place and sang in praise of the Lord of Tirukkaḻukkuṉṟam. To the further south of the Sankutīrtham tank stands the temple of Rudrakōṭi.[2] The place affords scope for enjoying a pleasant holiday.

PLACE NAME

The place names tell their own interesting story. Several factors have contributed to the naming of the villages in South India and of these the geographical or topographical location, flora or fauna of the area have been the most significant. There are a number of such places near Tirukkaḻukkuṉṟam named after trees, animals, birds etc. e.g. Ālappākkam is called after the banyan tree, Pulipākkam called after the tiger, Kunnapākkam called after the hillock. So, Tirukkaḻukkuṉṟam also seems to owe its name to this ancient practice that prevailed here. The original name Kalukkunram literally means 'Eagle hill' and prefix Tiru or Sacred should have been added after the place was sung by the Tevaram saints. There are quite a few places in Tamilnadu called after birds e.g. Mayilapūr and Mayilā)duturai (or Mayūram) after the peacock, Kaḷugumalai (eagle hill) near Koilpatti in Tirunelveli District.

The Sanskrit name Paksitīrtham also means the sacred place or tank of the birds. But the name is used by the learned few while Tirukkaḻukkuṉṟam is in popular usage. This name is however better known to the pilgrims of other parts of India.

The name *Vedagiri* is applied to the hill and the presiding deity of the temple is known as Vedagirīśvara. The Vedic association of Lord Siva is brought out by this name and there are quite a few places in South India with this name.

---

2 This temple is about a mile away and it is generally regarded as the most ancient one in this area; but the architectural features do not support this view. The principal deities worshipped here are Rudrakōṭīśvara and Abhirāmi Nāyaki. For legendary account connected with this place see infra,. Chapter 2 on Traditions of Tirukkaḻukkuṉṟam.

Vedāraṇyam and Vedarājapuram in Tanjavur District, Vedagiri and Vedachalam are popular names amongst the Śaiva inhabitants of Tirukkaḷukkuṉṟam.

COMMUNITIES

People of different castes and communities live in and around Tirukkaḷukkuṉṟam, like the Senkunra Mudaliars (predominantly weavers and landed gentry), Cheṭṭiars (traders), Vanniars, farmers who form the bulk, artisans and Śaiva Brahmins. Formerly, each community had its own quarters but in the recent years there is a greater inter-caste mobility. All of them hold the temples of their locality in high esteem and participate in the festivals and make their offerings.

ARCHAEOLOGY

That this area was occupied by the Megalithic folk during the onset of the Iron Age is attested by the existence of Megalithic monuments in and around Tirukkaḷukkuṉṟam. Thus, cairn-circles, a particular type of Megalithic tombs, are found at Rudrakōṭi (one mile east of Tirukkaḷukkuṉṟam), Oragaḍam, Pulikuṉṟam, Pūñjēri, Vellikuṉṟam, Mangalam, Ammaṇampākkam, Oṇḍivēḍu etc., and cist-type of Megalithic monuments, are found at Kuṉṉavākkam and Tiruppōrūr. The site at the latter place is protected by the Government of India as a monument of national importance. All the above-mentioned villages are in close vicinity of Tirukkaḷukkuṉṟam, and go to show that this area was humming with human activity in the Iron Age, to which the Megaliths have been ascribed, i.e., roughly between the third century B.C. and the first century A.D.[3]

Thus, the situation in an important position between Kāñci and Māmallapuram, and the sacredness of the Vedagiri hill and the temples, the beautiful natural landscape, the healthy climate of the place, have all contributed to make Tirukkaḷukkuṉṟam an attractive centre for pilgrims and tourists who come in large numbers on all days and particularly on Sundays and holidays.

---

3. *Ancient India,* Vol. V (1949), p. 42.

Chapter 2

LEGENDS AND TRADITIONS

The legends and traditions of a place or a temple were sought to be recorded in a class of literature called *Sthalapurāṇas* or *Mahatmiyams*. Almost all major temples of India have them. Not all of them however are of great antiquity. Mostly legendary or puranic in contents, they bristle with supernatural occurrences and characters and are of limited historical value. Their main purpose was to glorify the antiquity and the spiritual greatness of the temple and deities therein and also associate them with the holy rivers and venerable sages of the yore. Another method was to localise the epic and puranic stories like of the *Ramayana,* the *Mahabharata* or the Sivapuranas with the place. They follow a set pattern, as it were, and many episodes are replicated in several temples. It has been pointed out by scholars that the practice of writing the *Sthalapurāṇas* became popular during the 17th through 19th centuries, though a few of them could belong to an earlier period. It is futile to dissect them for historical gains except in rare cases. However, they are of value in the history of religious beliefs and rituals. Some festivals are conducted on the basis of the *Sthalapurāṇa* traditions and some sculptures also introduced to associate the legend with the temple.

To this category belongs the *Tirukkaḷukkuṉṟa Purāṇam,* available both in Tamil and Sanskrit. It has many chapters like Nandidēva-Sargam, Suraguṇa-Sargam, Vēdagiri-Sargam. They recount how Brahmā, Viṣṇu, Indra, Garuḍa had to come to Tirukkaḷukkuṉṟam and pay their obeisance to the Lord here and receive His blessings. According to this *purāna,* the Vedas prayed to Lord Śiva to make them more accessible to the people and, in answer to their prayers, he gave them a physical form of the hill and took his abode there. Hence, the hill here is named Vedagiri and the deity as Vedagirīsvara, the Hill of the Lord of the Vedas. There is also a popular legend that because the hills were regarded as the embodiment of the Vedas, the Śaiva saints did not go up the hill and they only worshipped from a place on the east of the hill now called Nālvar-Kōil (*Tirukkaḷukkuṉṟa-Ula,* Introduction by U.V. Swaminathaier, p. 17).

LEGENDS CONNECTED WITH THE TWO EAGLES

The Sanskrit *Sthalapurāṇa* calls this place Pakṣitīrtham[1] and Gangācalam while the Tamil purāṇa calls it Tirukkaḷuk-kuṉṟam.[2] There is a small tank on the hill which is identified as the holy tank of Pakṣitīrtham. Both the Purāṇas give the same version about the two eagles that are fed here, on the summit of the hill, every day (Fig. 6). According to them two eagles are associated with the place from the *Kṛta Yuga to Kali Yuga* and they visit the holy shrine on the hill in every *Yuga.*[3] The eagles ascribed to the *Kṛta Yuga* were *Caṇḍa* and *Pracaṇḍa.* These birds desired to attain spiritual bliss instead of the leadership of the bird kingdom and came to Tirukkaḷuk-kuṉṟam and worshipped Lord Vedagirīśvara on the hill. Lord Śiva being pleased by their sincere devotion made them the leaders of his personal attendants.

Jaṭāyu and Sampāti were the two eagles which worshipped Lord Śiva at the place during the *Trētha Yuga.* The traditional account is that there was a fight between the two birds, each claiming to be more powerful than the other. To test their power,

1. This refers to a small tank on the summit of the hill where two eagles are supposed to drink water after being fed by the priest. The place has been called Pakṣitīrtham, after the bird-tank on the hill.
2. The author of the Tamil Purāṇa says:
   "வடகலை யினெடுத்த கங்காசலபுரியைத் தென்னூலில்
   வகுத்துத் தொல்லோ ரினுடைய கழுக்குன்ற நகரமென."
3. Lines 9, 10 *Tirukkaḷukkuṉra Ula,* edited by Dr. U.V. Swaminathaier. Also Tirukkaḷukkuṉṟa Purāṇam: Gangācala Sadakam, Pūdāviruttha kathai. lines 8, 9.

they flew towards the sky from the top peak of the *Mēru*. A sage, by name Hamsa, saw them flying towards the sun and cursed them thinking that they intended to cause evil to the Sun God. Accordingly, Sampāti's wings were burnt and he fell on the Kalāyan mountains and Jaṭāyu fell on the Vindhyan mountains. They came to Tirukkaḷukkuṉṟam seeking redemption from the curse and prayed to Śiva. Śiva appeared before them and said that Jaṭāyu would be rid of his curse by rendering help to Sri Rāma in the Daṇḍakāraṇya forests, and that Sampāti would be freed on his helping Hanumān, while the latter was in search of Sīta, Rāma's wife.

Sambhuttan and Māhuttan are said to be two devotees associated with the *Dvāpara Yuga*. One was an ardent devotee of Lord Śiva and the other of Śakti. They began to quarrel over the superiority of their respective deities. Finally, they appealed to Lord Śiva himself to settle the dispute. Śiva appeared and told them that He and Śakti were one and inseparable. But they would not accept this and persisted in their quarrel. Śiva, it is said, became angry and cursed them to become eagles. They worshipped Him at Tirukkaḷukkuṉṟam and regained their original forms at the end of the Dvāpara Yuga.

During the *Kali Yuga,* Pūsha and Vidāthā, who were brothers, secluded themselves in a forest and to attain spiritual freedom did penance for a long time. When Śiva appeared before them they prayed to Him to grant *mōksha*. But Śiva who thought that they were yet unripe for such a state, asked them to wait and continue their penance for some more time. They became dissatisfied with Him and insisted that Śiva should grant them boon. Śiva could not tolerate this and cursed them. They were transformed into two eagles. He asked them to worship the Lord at Tirukkaḷukkuṉṟam and regain their original form at the end of the *Kali Yuga*. Thus, the two birds that visit this place today are considered to be the same old sinners! It is also believed that these birds would regain their original form at the end of this Yuga.

The popular version of this tradition is that these birds daily visit various holy temples like those at Kāśi and Rāmeśvaram. It is generally believed that they take their bath in the Ganges in the morning and worship in the temple and come to Tirukkaḷukkuṉṟam where they worship Lord Vedagirīśvara and take food. In the evening they proceed to Rāmeśvaram and worship the Lord there and reach Chidambaram in the night.[4]

This tradition must have been associated with Tirukkaḷukkuṉṟam from at least the 7th century A.D. for the Śaiva saints, Appar, Sambandar and Sundarar, about a century later, who visited and sang in praise of the Lord of Kaḷukkuṉṟam refer to this place, in their hymns, as Kaḷukkuṉṟam[5] (eagle-hill). It is probable that Appar and Sambandar had already heard about the sanctity of this shrine and the worship of the eagles there.

That this place was called by the name Kaḷukkuṉṟam after the 7th century is borne out by the devotional songs of the great Śaiva saints who had visited this place. Sundaramūrti Nāyanār who visited this place a century later than Appar and Sambandar, refers to it as Kaḷukkuṉṟam. Māṇikkavācakar also refers to this place as Kaḷukkuṉṟam in his devotional songs.[6] He is generally believed to have lived in the 9th century.

Another leading Śaiva saint to visit this place was Paṭṭi ṇattu Aḍigal, who lived in the 10th century A.D.[7] To him also this place was known as Kaḷukkuṉṟam. Aruṇagirināthar (15th century) in his *Tiruppugaḷ* refers to this place as Kaḷukkuṉṟam. Thus it is clear that from the 7th century to the present day this place has been called as Kaḷukkuṉṟam.

Apart from the literary sources, epigraphical sources also show that this place, throughout the ages, was known as Tirukkaḷukkuṉṟam. From the time of Narasimhavarman I[8] down to the days of the Vijayanagara Kings, i.e., from the 7th to

4. Though it cannot be ascertained whether these birds actually visit all the above said temples every day, it is mysterious enough to note that they visit Tirukkaḷukkuṉṟam almost every day at the appointed time, for the past many centuries.

5. *Tevāram:* Tirukkaḷukkuṉṟam -padikams of Appar, Sambandar and Sundarar.

6. *Tiruvācakam*: Tirukkaḷukkuṉṟam-padikam.

7. S. Anavaradavinayakam Pillai : *Tamil Perumakkal Varalāru,* pp. 192-194.

8. 65 of 1909.

the 16th century, all the epigraphs found here refer to this place as Kaḷukkuṉṟam and as situated in the subdivision named Kalattūr Kōṭṭam. During the Chola period, the place got an additional name Ulagananda Solapuram. But the original name Tirukkaḷukkuṉṟam had persisted.

Havart, a Dutch visitor, in his book *"Open Ondergang Van Coromandel"* published in 1693 says that he and ten others visited the hill on 3rd January, 1681 and saw two sacred birds feeding during the midday on that day.[9] It is of interest to note that the practice of the eagles visiting this place has continued at least from 1681 to this day, a period of about three centuries. This makes one think why it could not have been possible for the birds to have continued this practice even from the 7th century (as attested by the Tevaram hymns) or even earlier. Every day pilgrims visit the hill top to witness the grand sight of the two birds circling around the hill descend and sit by the side of the priest and take the sweet rice offered by him.

The *Sthalapurana* goes on to narrate in a very stereotyped manner how all the leading divinities like Brahmā, Viṣṇu, Indra, Nandi, Rudrakotis had to come to Kalukkunram to worship the Lord here and obtain redemption. It is said that Indra continues to pay obeisance to Vedagirisvara in the form of a thunderbolt, once in twelve years.[10]

Though it is not possible to ascertain how long these legends connected with Viṣṇu, Brahmā and Indra have been associated with Tirukkaḷukkuṉṟam, yet it can be said that these stories represent fanciful elaboration of the simple and conventional references in the hymns of Appar and Sundarar, who have stated in their hymns that Viṣṇu, Brahmā and Indra worshipped the Lord of Kaḷukkuṉṟam.[11] In one of the Tevaram hymns Appar says:

9. A.R.E. for 1909; p. 72.
10. This incident is referred to in a verse by Chokkanatha Pulavar; Tanippāḍartiraṭṭu – Part I (1953) Ed. by K. Subramania Pillai.
11. S.R. Namasivaya Rajayogi: *Tirukkaḷukkuṉṟam,* Introduction, p. xliv. According to the former trustee of the temple it is said to have been recorded by the temple authorities that two such instances took place in 1889 and 1901. It is generally believed that no damage was caused to the

பூவின் மேல் நான்முகனும் மாலும் போற்ற
புணர்வரிய பெருமானைப் புனிதன் தன்னைக்
காவலனைக் கழுக்குன்றம் அமர்ந்ததான் தன்னைக்
கற்பகத்தைக் கண்ணாரக் கண்டேன் நானே

and in another hymn,

"தேவார்ந்த தேவனைத் தேவரெல்லாம்
திருவடிமேல் அலரிட்டுத்தேடி நின்று
நாவார்ந்த மறை பாடி நட்டம் ஆடி
நான்முகனும் இந்திரனும் மாலும் போற்றக்
காவார்ந்த பொழிற்சோலைக் கானப் பேராய்
கழுக்குன்றத்துச்சியாய் கடவுளே..."

Sundarar also says:

"அந்தம் இந்தா அடியார்தம் மனத்தேயுறு
வந்து நாளும் வணங்கி மாலொடு நான்முகன்
சிந்தை செய்த மலர்கள் நித்தலுஞ் சேரவே
கந்தம் நாறும் புறவின் தண் கழக்குன்றமே"[12]

SANKU-TĪRTHAM (Sacred Conch Tank)

The next tradition in the *Sthalapurāṇas* is connected with the Sanku-tīrtham, which is down the hill on the south of the Vedagiri hill. Mārkaṇḍeya who visited this place came to the tank and found himself in need of a vessel for performing the *abhiṣeka* to Lord Śiva. He prayed to Lord Śiva and immediately a conch emerged from the tank with great noise and floated towards Mārkaṇḍeya, who picked it up and used it as a vessel for the purpose of doing *abhiṣeka* to Śiva. From this time onwards, it is said, there emerged from the tank a conch every twelve years.[13] It is said that the last two occasions on which such conches were gathered were July 18th, 1908 and June 26th, 1919.[14] Some of the conches that were taken from this tank are preserved in the temple even today. Every year on the last

---

temple on these occasions. In the Vedagirisvara temple on the summit of the hill, there is a hole in the roof. It is considered to be the spot through which the thunderbolt entered the shrine but disappeared miraculously without causing any damage! (I.A., Vol. X, p. 198)

12. Also see Tirukkaḷukkunṟa Ulā: Introduction by U.V. Swaminathaier, p. 17.
13. I.A. Vol.. X. p. 198.
14. *Tirukkaḷukkunṟa Purāṇam,* Chap. XXII, Suraguru sarga.

Monday of the month Kṛttikai the conches are used as vessels for *abhiṣeka.*

This tank is considered as one of the largest temple tanks of Tamilnadu. In the centre of the tank there is a beautiful *Nirāḷi maṇḍapa.* This tank gets its supply of water from the streams that flow down the hill, and it is generally believed that the water possesses curative powers.

The *Sthalapurāṇas* next give an account of Suraguru[15] claimed to be a Cōḷa king, who is said to have built the temple of Bhaktavatsala, below the hill. While the king was in the forest for hunt, he aimed an arrow at *Mayīgan,* who was in the form of a pig, but the arrow struck a cow and Tilōttama, who was cursed to be a cow by Nandi, regained her original form.

Suraguru wanted to inflict a suitable punishment on himself for killing a cow and was prepared to be crushed by the wheels of his own chariot.[16] But before he could kill himself, the sin escaped out of his body through the head in the form of a crow and fell on the south-west of the holy hill, Vedagiri! It is believed that it still remains there in the form of a hill, called Kākkaikuṉṟam. The people generally believe that this hill is a personification of sins and as a testimony to this, it remains barren with no trees growing on it, while the hills closeby are covered with bushes and trees.

The popular (but unhistorical) version of this tradition is that Suraguru built the Bhaktavatsala temple and was ruling Mahābalipuram. When he was out for hunt, he killed a porcupine near the sacred hill. Out of the dead animal came a Rākṣasa, who told him that he had been cursed by sage Mārkaṇḍeya and since then he had been waiting to be delivered by the king, It is also believed that on the same occasion the king had killed a cow by mistake and wanted to end his life by throwing himself under the wheels of his own chariot, as a

---

15. *Tirukkaḷukkuṉṟa Purāṇam, Ch*ap. XXII, Suraguru sarga.
16. This legend probably derives its origin from an accident that is believed to have occurred at Tiruvārūr in the Tanjore district during the period of Manu Cōḷa. It is well-known that a mother-cow of a dead calf trodden over by the prince in the course of a drive, complained of the offence to the king by ringing the bell fixed in front of the king's court. Manu killed his son by riding his own chariot on him as a punishment for the offence his son had committed.

punishment for his sin. When he was about to die, a beautiful damsel came out of the body of the dead cow.

There is also a representation of a dog, probably the dog of a minister of Suraguru, seeking its master. This, according to the local purāṇas, represents the dog of Suraguru's minister, which was found to be cured of its leprous sores because it had jumped into a tank near Vedagiri which possessed curative powers. The minister, it is said, who was also suffering from the same disease, saw this wonderful cure and bathed in the tank and got rid of his disease. How far it is historical is very difficult to say. But the fact that this place was used as a health resort by the Dutch Officers from the beginning of the 17th century,[17] goes to prove this to some extent. Now it is generally believed by the people that a stay here for about 40 days will cure any disease.[18]

There are a few more popular traditions, associated with this place. The most important of these is that connected with Sundaramūrti Nāyanār. Sundaramūrti, in the course of his pilgrimage in Toṇḍaimaṇḍalam, visited Tirukkaḷukkuṉṟam and prayed to Lord Śiva to give him some gold to meet his expenditure. Śiva promised to do so but wanted to delay and hide himself in the western *gōpura*. But Sundarar, who was searching for Śiva, entered the temple through the southern *gōpura*, he saw Lord Śiva hiding himself there, and prayed and got the gold he needed. On account of this, the deity in the lower temple came to be called as Poṉṉiṭṭanāthar.[19]

17. A.R.E. for 1909, p.121.

18. As a testimony to this we find a poem in *Kalugācala satagam* where the anonymous author says that he was cured of leprosy here at Tirukkaḷukkuṉṟam :

குடலொன்றிலே வலுரோகமாய்க்
குன்மம் மெனக் கன்மம் பிறந்
துடலொன்றிலே படும் வாதையை
உரை செய்ய வென் றரமோவையா
விடையொன்றிலே றிய தெய்வமே
விறல் பாடினாற் குறை தீருமே
கடலொன்றிலே விடமுண்டவா
கழுகாசலா கழுகாசலா

19. *Tirukkaḷukkunra Ulā*; Ed. by Swaminathier; p. 12. It is of interest to note that this incident is not referred to either in the local purāṇas or in the Periya Purāṇam, From epigraphical evidence it is possible for us to

In commemoration of this incident, a festival takes place in the Bhaktavatsala temple on the fourth day of the Brahmōtsava, when Lord Bhaktavatsala is represented as Ponniṭṭanāthar and taken in procession through the western *gōpura* and placed in a *maṇḍapa,* while Sundaramūrti Nāyanār, on an elephant *(vāhana),* is taken to the same *maṇḍapa* through the southern *gōpura.* It is supposed to represent the incident where the Nāyanār met Śiva and got gold from Him.

Another legend is connected with a dancing girl by name Nācimuttu. She was a great devotee of Śiva and she used to worship Him every day, singing a stanza from *Tirukkaḷukkuṉṟa Mālai* (திருக்கழுக்குன்ற மாலை), composed in praise of Lord Śiva. One day, it so happened that there was heavy rain and storm and she could not step out of her house. She was such a great devotee of Śiva, that when she prayed to Him to come down to her house and give *darśan,* He did so. She was very much pleased and when Śiva was about to leave her house she took hold of the feet of his *vāhana* (Nandi) and went along with Him to Kailāsa. It is also said that the author of the *Tirukkaḷukkuṉṟa Mālai* also took hold of her feet and reached Kailāsa with her. This tradition is referred to in many of the Tamil works like *Kshettirakkōvaip-piḷḷai Tamiḻ,*[20] *Tirukkaḷukkuṉṟa Ulā,*[21] *Kaḷukācala satagam*[22] and *Tirulingappadigam.*[23]

---

ascertain the association of the name with this place from the 13th century. An inscription of the 9th year of Jaṭāvarman Sundara Pāṇḍya I (1260) says that an officer of the Pāṇḍya king by name Kāman Araśan constructed the temple, the flower-garden and rows of houses round the shrine of Linga of Nāyanār Ponnittiśvaram Uḍaiyār, whom he consecrated (188 of 1894). The name of the deity, Ponnittiśvaram Uḍaiyār, suggests the origin of this tradition.

20. Tirukkaḷukkuṉṟa-Ula: Ed. by U.V. Swaminathaier, Introduction, pp. 14-16.
21. Ibid., lines 109; 353-54; 383-84.
22. Quoted by Swaminathaier; Introduction to Tirukkaḷukkuṉṟa-Ula, p.16.
23. S.R. Nāmasivayam, *Tirukkaḷukkuṉṟam* p. 286

முற்றத்திலே வந்து தாசி தமிழைக் கேட்டு
மோட்சங் கொடுத்த லிங்கம்

Tirulinga padikam, stanza II.

Thus a study of these legends shows that they are embodied in the Sthalapurāṇas because they exalt the sanctity of the temples at this place. These traditions were carried from time to time, in the minds of the people, for the past several centuries, with great belief in them. This shows how this had deeply influenced the religious attitude and piety of the people. The sectarian content of the legends is also very obvious.

Chapter 3

HISTORICAL BACKGROUND

The history of Tirukkaḷukkuṉṟam has been for a large part closely bound up with the history of Toṇḍaimaṇḍalam as a whole. Indeed, the numerous inscriptions found in the temples at Tirukkaḷukkuṉṟam may be said to contain a good record of the political history of Toṇḍaimaṇḍalam. They throw sufficient light on the chequered vicissitudes through which the place had to pass. They belong to many dynasties like the Pallava, Cōḷa, Rāṣṭrakūṭa, Pāṇḍya and the Vijayanagara, and clearly bring out the fluctuations in the political fortunes of this place.

Coming to historical times, the antiquity of Tirukkaḷukkuṉṟam in pre-Pallava days is not certain. We do not get any reference to the place in the whole of Śangam literature, though this negative evidence proves nothing. But we do get references to Toṇḍaimaṇḍalam of which this place also formed part. Toṇḍaimaṇḍalam which included the Chingleput district as a whole and the neighbouring districts of South and North Arcot, was, in ancient days, divided into two divisions, called Aruva South and Aruva North or Aruvānāḍu and Aruvāvaḍatalai-nāḍu respectively.[1] This region was noted even by Ptolemy, who called it as Aruvanoi.[2]

Toṇḍaimaṇḍalam was ruled by Toṇḍamān Iḷam Tiraiyan, a contemporary of Karikāla Cōḷa, ascribed to about the second

1. S. Krishnaswami Iyengar: J.I.H., II, p. 36 (The Aruvānāḍu was in the basin of the South Pennar and the Aruvāvadatalainādu lay further north in the basin of the Pālār).
2. K.N. Sivaraja Pillai : *Chronology of the Early Tamils,* pp. 227-28

century A.D. as it is known from one of the Śangam works, *Perumbāṇārruppadai*, written by Rudrankaṇṇṉār.[3] The poet mentions nothing specifically about the conquest of Tondaimandalam by Toṇḍamān Ilam Tiraiyan, but describes the conditions of Kāñci which was his capital, during his rule. It is quite possible that this region was called Toṇḍaimaṇḍalam after the name of ToṇḍamānIḷamTiraiyan.

From the inscriptions found at Tirukkaḷukkuṉṟam we know that this place formed part of Kaḷattūr kōṭṭam, which seems to have derived its name from a small village called Kaḷattūr (also known as Pon Viḷainda Kalattūr) about three miles south of the modern Chingleput town.[4]

UNDER THE PALLAVAS

It is however from the Pallava days that we get a clear picture of the history of this place. The long rule of the Pallavas for about six centuries or more, i.e., from the third to the ninth century, is generally divided into four periods, namely, the period of the copper-plate grants all in Prakrit dating from the time of Skandavarman; the period of the Pallavas of the copper plates all in Sanskrit; the period of the Pallavas of the stone inscriptions when the Śimhavisnu line became prominent and the period of the new line of the Pallavas under Nandivarman Pallavamalla.[5] The Prakrit and Sanskrit copper plates throw very little light on the political history of the area.[6]

The stone inscriptions are of great value and they throw welcome light on the political history.

SKANDAŚIṢYA

The earliest Pallava king to be associated with Tirukkaḷukkuṉṟam is Skandaśiṣya, who is mentioned in the inscription of Āditya I[7] as a former Pallava king, who made a grant to the Mūlasthana temple at Tirukkaḷukkuṉṟam. The late Venkayya identified this Skandaśiṣya with Skandavarman.[8] But, as there

3. K.A. Nilakanta Sastri: *Studies in the Cola History and Administration*, pp. 17-52.
4. S.I.I., III, p. 143; I.A., XXI, p. 197, note 1.
5. K.A. Nilakanta Sastri: *A Short History of South India*, pp. 97-98.
6. *Ibid.*, p. 99.
7. 167 of 1894.
8. *Ep. Ind.*, Vol. III, p. 276.

are many Skandavarmans in the Pallava records, it was difficult for him to identify the exact ruler mentioned in the inscription. Dubreuil places him roughly in the middle of the 5th century (i.e., 450 A.D.) as his name is found mentioned in the Velurpalayam plates of Nandivarman between Virakurca and Kumāraviṣṇu and also by the support derived from the Vayalur record.[9] It is clear from this that the place was already celebrated so as to attract the grant of Skandaśiṣya.[10]

The emergence of a new line of Pallavas beginning with Simhaviṣṇu (575-600 A.D.), called the Great Pallavas, marks a new epoch in the history of the Pallava power. From this period onwards the Pallava authority begins to penetrate much farther into the Tamil country than before.[11] During this period a beginning was made in Tamil land to excavate cave temples. Inscriptions of the Pallava kings are found in these temples. The earliest inscriptions dated in the reign of Mahēndravarman I are found in the Chingleput, South Arcot and Trichinopoly districts. One of Mahēndravarman I's cave temples with his inscriptions is found at Vallam near Tirukkaḷukkuṉṟam.[12]

Mahēndravarman I was followed by Narasimhavarman I. There is a rock-cut *maṇḍapa* called *orukal maṇḍapa,* a little below the main temple on the hill, Vēdagiri. It is suggested that this monolithic cave might, in all probability, have been excavated in the time of Narasimhavarman I[13] as there is an inscription[14] of Narasimhavarman at the top of the second pillar, recording the gift made by him to the God of the Mūlasthāna on the sacred hill (Srimalai-mil) at this place. This inscription mentions his coveted title *'Vatāpi-Konda'* (who took Vatapi) at the end. It also records that Tirukkaḷukkuṉṟam formed part of Kaḷattūrkōṭṭam.

9. According to Krishna Sastri the Skandaśisya of the Velurpalayam plates, son of Virakurca, is perhaps identical with the Skandaśisya of the Tirukkaḷukkuṉṟam inscription and placed in 358 A.D. See also J.M.U., XIV, p. 19.
10. This Skandaśiṣya has been identified with one Skandasēna who is said to have excavated the rock-cut temple at Vallam near Chingleput.. (S.I.I., XII, Introduction, page II). But the identification is not quite convincing, as the editor of the S.I.I. XII himself admits.
11. R. Gopalan: *History of the Pallavas of Kānci,* p. 79.
12. The cave temple at Vallam is called Vasantēśvara cave.
13. *A.R.E.* for 1909, p. 75 & *Ancient India,* XIV, pp. 119-20.
14. 65 of 1909; *A.R.E.* for 1932-33, p. 55.

Unfortunately, this inscription does not say who excavated the *orukal maṇḍapa* or any other information about it. But the title 'Vatāpi koṇḍa' confirms the fact that it belongs to Narasimhavarman I, who defeated the western Calukyas and captured their capital, Vatapi, i.e., Badami in 642 A.D.[15] This inscription must have been engraved in or after 642. But this does not mean that this place came under his rule only in 642 or a little later. As we have already seen, this place was under the Pallavas as early as the 4th or 5th century.

Though this *maṇḍapa* is in the Mahēndra style, it was excavated by Narasimhavarman I, as the successors of Mahēndra continued to excavate similar temples initiated by Mahēndra.[16] The existence of Narasimhavarman I's inscription in this temple helps us in coming to this conclusion.

It is quite probable that this inscription was engraved on the cave temple to commemorate the heroic victory of Narasimhavarman I over Pulakēsin II, the Cāḷukya ruler, and the capture of Vātāpi by the former. This was the outcome of the mutual conflict among the Pallavas of Kāñci and the Cāḷukyas of Vātāpi, "each seeking constantly to extend its empire at the expense of its neighbour".[17]

PARAMEŚVARAVARMAN I

Narasimhavarman I died about 668 A.D. and in Paramēśvaravarman I's reign certain improvements were made in the temple architecture. Attempts were made to construct structural *vimānas,* having stone as the building material. As pointed out by K.R. Srinivasan, for the first time, entire granite slabs were

15. *S.I.I.*, II, pp. 508-09, translation.

16. K.R. Srinivasan: *Ancient India,* XIC, p. 118. According to Longhurst this *mandapa* was excavated in the reign of Mahendravarman I and the inscription of Narasimhavarman was added to it later, along with the sculptures of Brahmā and Viṣṇu, which resemble in style the later sculptures of the same deities adorning the temples of Mamalla period *(Annual Report of the Dept. of Archaeology, Southern Circle for 1919-20,* part II, pp. 2-25).

17. K.A. Nilakanta Sastri: *op. cit,.* p. 141. By this victory Narasimhavarman I took revenge on the Calukyas for their early victory over his father, Mahendravarman I and capture of the northern provinces of the Pallavas.

used to build temples in a dolmenoid fashion. The central shrine of the Vēdagirīśvara temple on the hill at Tirukkaḷukkuṉṟam is built of three huge slabs of stone forming its inner walls with a roof-slab on top. These slabs are covered externally by the moulded stonework of the later Cōḷa times. Internally, the inner surfaces of the slabs enclosing the cella have on them the characteristic bas-relief sculptures of Sōmāskanda, on the back-wall[18] and Dakṣiṇāmūrti, Nandi, Caṇḍikēśvara etc. on the other walls, indicating the period of Paramēśvara I.[19]

This dolmenoid structure evidently replaced the brick and-mortar *Mūlasthāna* temple of Skandaśiṣya Pallava.[20] Thus, the existence of this temple shows that this place received the patronage of the Pallava king, Paramēśvaravarman I.

UNDER THE CŌḶAS

ĀDITYA I (871-907)

The reign of Aparājita witnessed the collapse of the Pallava power. The neighbouring powers gained strength at the expense of the Pallava power. The Cōḷas under Āditya I came to prominence and occupied certain portion of the Pallava dominion.[21] Moreover, he gained the southern portion of Toṇḍaimaṇḍalam as a prize for the help he had rendered to the Pallavas against the Pāṇḍyan king, Varaguṇa II, in the battle of Srīpurāmbiyam.[22] Encouraged by this, Āditya began to make considerable inroads into the Pallava country and ultimately defeated Aparājita[23] and brought about the conquest of

---

18. It was the practice to have the image of Sōmāskanda sculpture on the back wall of the *garbagraha,* behind the main Siva shrine. That this feature was commonly adopted in the Pallava times is well attested to by Dubreuil in his Iconography of South India, p. 34 where he says; "The image of Sōmāskanda is the great master designer of Pallava iconography; it seems that it represents the essential part of Pallava Saivism about 700 A.D., for the image is usually formed in front of the Lingam, on the wall which forms the back of the sanctuary."
19. K.R. Srinivasan; *Ancient India,* XIV, p. 132.
20. *Ibid.*
21. *Ep. Ind.,* Vol. XXIII, p. 146.
22. *S.I.I.,* Vol. II, p. 384, Verse 18 (Udayendiram Plates).
23. *S.I.I.,* Vol. III, Tiruvālangādu & Kanyakumari Inscriptions.

Toṇḍaimaṇḍalam. This is clearly brought out by his inscriptions found at Tirukkaḷukkunṟam.[24] It is dated in the 27th regnal year of Āditya and refers to a grant made by Skandaśiṣya, the Pallava king, to the God at the place which was renewed by Vātāpi konda Narasimhavarman I, the Pallava ruler, and again renewed by Āditya. "Such a renewal is normal after a conquest and as Āditya I is known to have conquered the Pallavas and annexed Toṇḍaimaṇḍalam to the Cōḻa country, it is practically certain that the inscription is one of Āditya's."[25] It is not possible to ascertain how long he ruled after the date of this inscription. It is possible to presume that the conquest of Toṇḍaimaṇḍalam by Āditya was effected rather late in his reign.[26]

PARĀNTAKA I (907-955)

As soon as Parāntaka I came to the throne, he invaded the Pāṇḍya country and captured Madura and assumed the title *Maduraikoṇḍa*. An inscription of his 13th regnal year is found at this place,[27] indicating that the locality had come under his sway. This inscription records a gift of one lamp to the God of the holy Mūlasthāna by one Nedumāl Sattan Sennippērayan of Karaikkāṭṭūr in Amūr kōṭṭam and his mother.[28]

But the Cōḻa power under Parāntaka I witnessed a breakdown for a moment. Towards the end of his reign, the Rāṣṭrakūṭas under Kṛṣṇa III invaded the Cōḻa country and occupied a large part of the northern half of it, after his victory over the Colas in the Battle of Takkōlam,[29] six miles to the south-east of Arakonam, in 949 A.D. There are two inscriptions at Tirukkaḷukkunṟam belonging to Kṛṣṇa III. The inscription[30] of the 17th year of Kṛṣṇa III with the title "He who captured Kāñci and Tanjore" (*Kachiyum Tanjaiyum konda*) shows that he had seized the principal cities of the Cōḻa kingdom after the battle of Takkōlam. There is also another inscription of the 19th year of Kṛṣṇa III.[31] The existence of these inscriptions indicates that this place came under his sway.

24. 168 of 1894; *Ep. Ind.*, III, p. 280.
25. K.A. Nilakanta Sastri, *The Colas*, p. 111.
26. R. Gopalan; *op. cit.*, p. 143.
27 168 of 1894; *Ep. Ind.*, III, p. 280.
28. *Ibid.*
29. K.A. Nilakanta Sastri; *A History of South India*, pp.169-70.
30. 169 of 1894; *Ep. Ind.*, III, p. 282.
31. 170 of 1894.

RĀJĒNDRA I (1012-1044)

When Rājēndra I succeeded Rājarāja I the Cōḷa empire was the most extensive and most respected state of his time. By this time the bulk of Toṇḍaimaṇḍalam was recovered by the Cōḷas from the Rāṣṭrakūṭas and the Cōḷa empire extended upto Nellore as in the days of Parāntaka I.[32] An inscription of his 16th regnal year is found in this place recording a gift of a lamp to the temple.[33] This shows that Tirukkaḷukkuṉṟam did not fail to receive his patronage. There is an inscription dated in the 42nd year of Kulōttunga I[34] referring to a grant of 10 *Kāśu* to the temple at Tirukkaḷukkuṉṟam by an inhabitant of Rājarāja-puram which was utilised by the temple authorities to purchase some land for maintaining the *matha* of Naminandi Adigal[35] at Tirukkaḷukkuṉṟam. The endowed lands were in the village of Vānavan Mādēvi-Caturvēdimangalam.[36] The village Rājarāja-puram was evidently named after Rājarāja the great.[37] It is interesting to note that one of Rājēndra's queens was called Vānavan Mahādēvi and the village mentioned in the inscrip-tion must have been re-named after her name.[38] These evidences show that Tirukkaḷukkuṉṟam received his patronage.

RĀJĀDHIRĀJA I (1018-54) TO VĪRARĀJĒNDRA

The period between Rājādhirāja I and Vīrarājēndra was one of conflict between the Cōḷas and the Cāḷukyas. Rājādhirāja I defeated the Western Cāḷukyas and sacked their capital Kalyāṇi and assumed the title 'Vijayarājēndra'. But in 1050, the Cōḷas were driven out of the Cāḷukya empire by Somēśvara I. Rājā-dhirāja, along with his younger brother Rājēndra II (1052-64), had to attack the Cāḷukyas for a second time. In the battle of Koppam the Cōḷas emerged victorious but Rājādhirāja died in

32. K.A.N. Sastri; *The Cōlas*, p. 178.
33. 171 of 1894; *S.I.I.*, Vol. V. No. 464, p. 181.
34. 179 of 1894; *S.I.I.*, Vol. III, Part II, p. 164. This village was in Kirappakkam in modern Chingleput taluk.
35. Naminandi-Adigal is one of the 63 devotees of Śiva, whose lives are described in the *Periya Purāṇam* work of the 12th century (*I.A.*, XXI, p. 281).
36. *S.I.I.*, Vol. III, No. 75, p. 164. This village was in Kirappakkam in modern Chingleput taluk.
37. Dadapuram near Villupuram was originally Rājarājapuram
38. Compare Seramadevi near Tirunelveli.

the battle.[39] Rājēndra II crowned himself on the battlefield and marched to Kollāpura (Kolhapur) and planted there a pillar of victory. He had also to face the Western Cāḷukyas in order to prevent them from intervening in the affairs of the Eastern Cāḷukyas. There are inscriptions at Tirukkaḷukkuṉṟam of Rājādhirāja I[40] and Rājēndra II.[41] Rājādhirāja II was succeeded by Vīrarajēndra whose inscription is also found at this place.[42]

KULŌTTUNGA I (1070-1120)

After Rājēndra I, the next Cōḷa emperor to figure prominently in the history of Tondaimandalam was Kulōttunga I. He was the first Cāḷukya Cōḷa Emperor, who had married the daughter of Rājēndra II. Kulōttunga infused fresh vigour into the imperial power and undertook several campaigns and concentrated his efforts on the strengthening of his empire in the south and west. The inscription at Tirukkaḷukkuṉṟam[43] furnishes the details regarding his southern campaigns. It states how Kulōttunga defeated and drove away "the five Pandyas", seized the pearl fisheries as well as Podiyil region and burnt Koṭṭāru. Literary sources also corroborate this version. The *Vikramaśōḷa Ulā* confirms the above version and the *Kalingattupparaṇi* gives the additional fact that Vilinjam and Kanḍalūr Śālai were destroyed by him.[44] Up to 1115, the Cōḷa empire under Kulōttunga I remained intact except for the loss of Ceylon which asserted its independence. But, towards the end of the reign, he met with troubles from Mysore and Vengi under Vikramāditya. Thus, Kulōttunga sustained another curtailment of his empire which by the end of his reign was practically confined to the Tamil country and relatively small area of the adjoining Telugu district.[45] His inscriptions found at the place range from his 14th year to 47th year and this shows clearly that this place formed part of his empire throughout his long reign.

39. *Ep. Ind.*, XII, pp. 296-98.
40. 172 of 1894; *S.I.I.*, V. No. 465.
41. 173 of 1894; *S.I.I.*, V., No. 466 & 128 of 1932-33.
42. 175 of 1894; *S.I.I.*, V., No. 468.
43. *S.I.I.*, III, No. 69, pp.143-47. There are altogether five inscriptions of Kulōttunga I at this place. 174, 179, 189 of 1894, 124 and 137 of 1932-33.
44. *S.I.I.*, III, No. 69.
45. K.A.N. Sastri: *A History of South India*, p. 184.

VIKRAMA CŌḶA (1118-35) TO RĀJĒNDRA III (1246-79)

Vikrama Cōḷa, who succeeded Kulōttunga I, undertook the task of recovering Vengi and Gangavāḍi but was successful in getting back Vengi. Two of his inscriptions, dated in his third and 15th regnal years,[46] are found at this place. Kulōttunga II (1133-50) came to the Cōḷa throne next and ten of his inscriptions are found here,[47] ranging from his 3rd to the 12th year and usually begin with *'Pūmēivaḷara'* etc. and mentioning the title Tribuvana Cakravartin. Next Rājarāja II (1146-73) came to the throne and he was succeeded by Rājādhirāja II.[48] During Rājādhirāja II's reign (1163-79) a fierce succession dispute broke out in the Pāṇḍya empire and it forced him to intervene in the Pāṇḍyan affairs with disastrous effects. "Out of the ashes of the civil war arose the Pāṇḍya power which in its renewed strength soon swallowed the Cōḷas..."[49] The processes of dismemberment continued in the reign of the next Cōḷa ruler. Kulōttunga III (1178-1816) who succeeded Rājādhirāja II was the last great Cōḷa emperor. In the beginning of his reign, success favoured him and he put Vikrama Pāṇḍya, his ally, on the Pāṇḍyan throne. But his interference in the Pāṇḍyan civil war proved to be disastrous when Māravarman Sundar Pāṇḍya undertook the war of reprisal against Kulōttunga III and defeated him. This was one of the fiercest invasions of the Cōḷa empire causing considerable loss of life and property. Kulōttunga III sought refuge in flight and the situation was saved by the timely intervention of the Hoyśāḷas with whom the Cōḷa king had friendly relationship.

There are eight inscriptions of Kulōttunga III at this place. In three of them, Kulōttunga is referred to as one "who was pleased to take Madurai and the crowned head of the Pāṇḍya."[50] This title probably refers to the humiliation of the Pāṇḍya ruler Jaṭāvarman Kulaśēkhara in 1205, the rival candidate of Vikrama Pāṇḍya, whom Kulōttunga put on the Pāṇḍyan throne. Other five inscriptions at this place give Kulōttunga the

46. 176 of 1894; *S.I.I.*, Vol. V, No. 469, p. 185, & 127 of 1932-33.
47. 138, 140, 142, 146, 155, 157, 162, 163, 186 of 1932 - 33.
48. 183 of 1894; *S.I.I.*, V, No. 476 & 123, 159, 184 of 1932-33.
49. K.A.N. Sastri; *op. cit.*, p. 186 & *The Cōḷas*, pp. 354 and 366.
50. 133, 136, 163 of 1932-33.

title of Tribuvana Cakravarti, Tribuvanavīradēva and "who, having taken Madurai, Īḷam, Karuvūr and the Crowned head of the Pāṇḍya, was pleased to perform the anointment of heroes and of victors."[51] That Kulōttunga's activities extended to this place is evident from the existence of these inscriptions here and from the re-naming of Olukarai as Kulōttunga-Śōḷa-nallūr in Māttūr nāḍu in Jayangoṇḍa-Śōḷa-Maṇḍalam.[52] It is also of interest to note that one entire Kōṭṭam (Puliyūr Kōṭṭam) was named after him as Kulōttunga-Śōḷa-Vaḷanāḍu in one of the inscriptions.[53]

Kulōttunga III was succeeded by Rājarāja III (1216-46)[54] and in his reign confusion became more confounded and it hastened the decline and dissolution of the Cōḷa empire. Internal disorder and the desire of the local chieftains to assert their independence and the defiance of the king's orders became common features of the history of the Cōḷa country. Added to this, Rājarāja III continued the fight against the Pāṇḍyan ruler, Sundara Pāṇḍya. Rājarāja III was imprisoned by Kōpperuñjinga, the Kāḍava chieftain, an ally of the Pāṇḍyan ruler. But Narasimha II, the Hoyśāḷa king, an ally of the Cōḷa king, promptly came to his rescue and restored him to liberty and put him on the Cōḷa throne. The Pāṇḍyan king was also defeated by Narasimha II and was forced to consent to the restoration of Rājarāja III to the Cōḷa throne.

Rājēndra III (1246-79) succeeded Rājarāja III. He made strenuous efforts to revive the lost prestige and power of the Cōḷas. The rivalry between the Cōḷas and the Pāṇḍyas continued even in his reign, resulting in the decisive defeat of the Cōḷas at the hands of the Pāṇḍyan ruler Māravarman Pāṇḍya and later at the hands of Jaṭāvarman Sundara Pāṇḍya I (1251-61), "One of the most famous warriors and conquerors of South India under whom the Pāṇḍyan power attained its greatest splendour." The Cōḷa empire ceased to exist and was completely absorbed into the Pāṇḍyan empire.

51. 121, 144, 145, 149, 153 of 1932-33.
52. 163 of 1932-33.
53. 149 of 1932-33.
54. 131, 143, 158, 161, 166, 164 of 1932-33.

UNDER THE KĀḌAVARĀYAS

KŌPPERUÑJINGA

The Kāḍavarāyas came to prominence in the first half of the 13th century and became an independent power under Kōpperuñjinga, though only for a short time. Kōpperuñjinga was a subordinate of the Cōḷas in charge of the South Arcot region, with his headquarters at Sendamangalam. Rājarāja III's weak rule gave him an opportunity to make inroads into the Cōḷa territory. He joined the Pāṇḍyan ruler, Māravarman Sundara I, and defeated and captured the Cōḷa king — Rājarāja II. But soon he was defeated by the Hoyśāḷa king, Narasimha in 1230-31, who forced him to accept the overlordship of the Cōḷas. This was only for a short time, for, we find the appearance of his inscriptions with his own regnal years, which clearly shows that he became more or less an independent ruler.[55] Later on, he defeated the Hoyśāḷas under Vīra Sōmeśvara and also proceeded against the Kākātiyas, who had occupied the region as far south as Kāñci. In the war that took place between Kōpperuñjinga and the Kākātiyas, the former was helped by his son, Kāḍavan Kumaran who was probably ruling over the region consisting of Mahabalipuram and Kāñci, that is, a part of Toṇḍaimaṇḍalam.[56] How far Kōpperuñjinga was successful against the Kākātiyas is not known. But the region over which he had direct control included the modern districts of South and North Arcot and a part of the Chingleput district.[57] The existence of his inscriptions at Tirukkaḷukkuṉṟam[58] clearly shows that this place came under his rule. In all probability, it was under the rule of his son, Kāḍavan Kumaran, who might have acted as his representative over this part of Toṇḍaimaṇḍalam.

Kōpperuñjinga was decisively defeated by Jaṭāvarman Sundara Pāṇḍya in about 1264. From then he became a feudatory under the Pāṇḍyas. With his death the Kāḍava power came to an end.

55. K.A. Nilakanta Sastri, *The Cōḷas*, p. 430.
56. *J.M.U.*, X, p. 56. K.V. Raman, *The Early History of Madras Region*. Ch. II.
57. *Ibid.*, p. 63.
58. 181, 189A, 189B of 1894; *S.I.I.*, V, Nos. 474, 488, 486 & 148, 160 of 1932-33.

UNDER THE ŚAMBŪVARĀYAS

Like the Kāḍavarāyas, the Śambūvarāyas were originally feudatories of the Cōḷas and came to prominence by asserting their independence during the weak rule of the last Cōḷa kings. The origin of this dynasty is not clear. We find references made to some chiefs of this dynasty in the inscription of Vikrama-cōḷa.[59] An inscription at Tirukkaḻukkuṉṟam dated in the 6th year of Kulōttunga II mentions one Ediriliśōḷa-Śambūvarāya, 'one who had no enemies', who presided over a committee to pass judgement over a case of murder.[60] This shows that the Śāmbūvarāyas were subordinate to the Cōḷas in the reign of Kulōttunga II.

Chingleput district, along with South and North Arcot districts, was under their control till the establishment of the Vijayanagara rule over this region. Two of the inscriptions of the Śambūvarāya chief, Rājanārāyaṇa Śāmbūvarāya[61] (1337-62) are found at Tirukkaḻukkuṉṟam and this shows that this place received the patronage of the chiefs.

But the Śambūvarāya chiefs could not check the extension of the Vijayanagar rule into the Tamil country. In the reign of Kampaṇa II, the Śambūvarāyas were defeated and this "automatically extended the Vijayanagara empire as far as the South Arcot district in the South." The threat of the Muslim penetration in the South also necessitated the establishment of the strong Vijayanagara empire in the South, which united the Tamil country and gave a benevolent government to it.

UNDER THE PĀṆḌYAS

JAṬĀVARMAN SUNDARA PĀṆḌYA

As mentioned earlier, Jaṭāvarman Sundara Pāṇḍya I became the ruler of the whole of the Cōḷa empire in about 1264 A.D. Kāñci became another capital of the Pāṇḍyan kingdom. Four of his inscriptions are found at Tirukkaḻukkuṉṟam.[62] One of them[63] refers to an interesting information that in the 9th year of his reign, an officer by name Kāman Arasan or Adiyaman-

---

59. *Ep. Ind.*, XXVIII, p. 155 & K.A.N. Sastri: *op. cit.*, p.403.
60. 162 of 1932-33.
61. 178 of 1894; *S.I.I.*, V, No. 471 & 61 of 1909.
62. 186, 187, 188 of 1894; *S.I.I.*, V, No. 480, 481, 482, 147 of 1932-33.
63. 188 of 1894 & *J.M.U.*, XIV, pp. 19-20.

dēvar, constructed a shrine, the flower-garden and rows of houses round the shrine of Nāyanār Ponnittīśvaram-Uḍaiyār. It is quite probable that this deity may be the Bhaktavatsalēśvara of modern times. This part of the Pāṇḍyan empire went into the hands of the Śambūvarāyas, before it was conquered by the Vijayanagar ruler Kampaṇa II.

UNDER THE VIJAYANAGAR RULERS

The first Vijayanagar ruler to be associated with Tirukkaḻukkunṟam was Bukka I (1346-1377). It was in his reign that the Śambūvarāyas were overthrown and the Tamil land was captured and included in the Vijayanagara empire by Kampaṇa II. Kampaṇa II was the son of Bukka I, in charge of the Southern part of the empire. That this place had received the patronage of these two, is known from the existence of their inscriptions at this place.[64] The inscription of Bukka I records an interesting information that certain provision was made to the temple for performing worship to god by the *Ūravar, Paradēśis* and *Nānādēśis* of Caduravācagan-paṭṭinam (Sadras) from the income collected as duties on some articles of merchandise. It is of interest to note that the mention of *Paradēśis* and *Nānādēśis* testifies to the activity of the merchants from several countries settled here.

Bukka I was succeeded by his son Harihara II (1377-1404) who consolidated the authority of Vijayanagara over Southern India. Though we have no inscription of Harihara II at Tirukkaḻukkunṟam, we have four inscriptions of his son,[65] Virūppaṇa-Uḍaiyar (Virupanna) who was the governor of the Tamil country from 1380 onwards. He might have succeeded to the power and influence of Kampaṇa II.[66] His inscriptions at this place are dated in 1388 A.D.

The Vijayanagara ruler who figures next is Bukka II (1405-06). Two inscriptions of Bukka II[67] are found at this place. One of them[68] records a festival called *Bokkaṟāyan-Sandi,* probably

64. Bukka I; 173 of 1932-33; Kampaṇa II; 185 of 1894 & 170 of 1932-33.
65. 171, 172, 174, 175 of 1932-33.
66. N. Venkataramanayya; *Vijayanagara, Origin of the City and the Empire,* p. 126.
67. 57, 58 of 1909.
68. 57 of 1909.

named after the king. It shows that Bukka might have visited the temple at this place and in all probability, this festival was inaugurated in the year of his visit to the temple.

Bukka II was soon ousted from power by Dēvarāya I[69] (1406-22) who was succeeded by Dēvarāya II in about 1426. His inscription at this place records the title "He who witnessed the elephant hunt" which probably refers to his victories over the enemy kings who were strong as elephants.[70]

During all these reigns, the hostility between the Vijayanagara and the Bāhmini kingdoms was a common feature. When Kṛṣṇadēvarāya (1509-30) came to the throne, the political fortunes favoured the Vijayangara empire and it once again extended all over South India. An inscription of Kṛṣṇadēvarāya at Tirukkaḷukkuṉṟam[71] shows that his authority extended over this place and it did not fail to receive his patronage.

After Kṛṣṇadēvarāya's time, this place was rather uninterrupted by the political factors and was perhaps left to the care of private donors, who took care of the temples as well as the village. One Pēramabala Tambiran is said to have taken great interest in the temples at this place and successfully made this place what it is now, viz., one of the most popular places in South India.[72]

The history of this place after the 16th century, as said in the beginning of the chapter, was closely bound up with the history of Chingleput, because it was not a place of any strategic importance. In the later half of the 17th century, Tirukkaḷukkuṉṟam was used as a health resort by the Dutch, who had settled in Sadras. Many of the Dutch governors and chiefs of Settlements visited this place and the hill, Vedagiri. We have numerous names of these Dutch visitors, along with the years of their visit, inscribed on the walls of the *orukal maṇḍapa*, and these years range between 1664 and 1687.[73] Moreover, we have an account of a Dutch visitor, Havart, who in his book *"Open Ondergang Van Coromandel"* published in 1693, says that

69. 177 of 1894; *S.I.I.*, V. No. 470 & *J.M.U.*, XIV, pp. 19-20 Appendix.
70. 64 of 1909; *S.I.T.I.*, Vol. I, p. 465.
71. 130 of 1932-33.
72. *I.A.*, X, p. 198.
73. *A.R.E.* for 1909, pp. 121-22.

on the 3rd of January, 1681 he and ten other Dutchmen visited the hill at this place and saw two sacred kites being fed by a priest at about noon on that day.[74]

In the 18th century, the history of this place was marked by the invasion of the Carnatic by Haidar Ali of Mysore in 1780. A large number of villages round Madras were burnt and devastated by his troops.[75] A record of the temple at Tirukkaḷukkuṉṟam says that during the raid of Haidar Ali, a portion of the Bhaktavatsala temple was destroyed and two of the conches, which were recovered from the *Sankutīrtham* tank, were taken away.[76] In the 19th century, certain repairs and construction of new *maṇḍapas,* e.g., the *maṇḍapa* in front of the Tripurasundari Śhrine, were made.

74. *A.R.E.* for 1909, pp. 72-73.

75. *Imperial Gazetteer of India*, Provincial Series, Madras, pp.18-23.

76. *Tirukkaḷukkuṉṟa Kōil Purvottaram* (Oriental Manuscripts Library, Madras).

Chapter 4

TEMPLES OF TIRUKKAḺUKKUṈṞAM – ORIGIN AND GROWTH

The origins of institutions of hoary past are generally shrouded in mystery and it is so particularly with the ancient temples of South India. To get at the historical origins of them, inscriptions found in them are of great value. Though the inscriptions do not very often help us in fixing the exact date of the origins of the temples, yet they help us in fixing the upper limits of their date.[1] Where we do not find any inscription to come to our aid in fixing the date, the architectural features of the construction are always of great help to throw some light on the date of such buildings.

Inscriptions found in the Tirukkaḷukkuṉṟam temples belonging to various dynasties like the Pallavas, Rāṣṭrakūṭas, Cōḷas, Pāṇḍyas and the Vijayanagara kings give information about the construction of various shrines and mandapas during different periods. The earliest extant temple in Tirukkaḷukkuṉṟam belongs to the 7th century A.D.[2] and it is in the rock-cut cave temple named Orukal Mandapa halfway up the hill.

1 K.K. Pillay: *The Sucindram Temple*, p. 111.
2 65 of 1909; *A.R.E.* for 1932-33, p. 55.

THE EARLIEST TEMPLE AT TIRUKKAḶUKKUṈṞAM ASSOCIATED WITH SKANDAŚIṢYA

The earliest reference to the existence of a temple at Tirukkaḷukkuṉṟam is however found in an inscription of Āditya I.[3] It refers to an endowment granted to Sri Mūlasthānattupperumānaḍigaḷ by the Pallava king Skandaśiṣya (Skandavarman), which was later on renewed by Narasimhavarman I and still later by Āditya I himself, for the second time. This leads us to the inference that there must have been in existence at Tirukkaḷukkuṉṟam a temple during the time of Skandaśiṣya, i.e., the 5th century A.D. much earlier than the cave temple, i.e., Orukal Mandapa. But it is not possible for us now, with the materials available, to say with any certainty where this temple existed and in what shape.

We know from one of the inscriptions of Mahendra Varman I[4] that temples existed even before his time and they were built of brick, timber, metal and mortar. This disproves the view that Mahendravarman was the first king to introduce the art of temple building into South India.[5] After this inscription had come into light, it is generally accepted by all authorities that what Mahendravarman I actually did was to substitute imperishable material (stone) in place of the perishable materials used till his time.

According to J. Dubreuil, "at the epoch of Mahendra it is certain that there did exist temples of stone, brick, timber, metal and mortar, and that these buildings made of perishable materials have all fallen into ruins, and have been destroyed by time."[6]

Longhurst also agrees with this view. According to him Mahendra was "the inventor or originator of the art of carving Hindu temples out of natural rocks instead of building them in

3. 167 of 1894; *Ep. Ind.*, III, p. 276.
4. The Mandagappattu inscription runs as follows: "this is the temple caused to be constructed by the king Vichitra Chitta for Brahmā, Īśvara and Vishṇu, without (the use of) brick, timber, metal and mortar."
5. N. Venkataramanayya: *An Essay on the Origin of the South Indian Temple,* pp 61-62.
6. J. Dubreuil; *op. cit.*

the usual way with bricks and lime, wooden pillars and roofs decorated with metal finials."[7]

Gopinatha Rao says, "the statement made in this inscription (Mandagappattu inscription) that Mahendravarman did not employ brick, metal, etc., clearly warrants our drawing the conclusion that temples built before his time were all of such perishable materials as brick, etc."[8]

To support this view, we have the epigraphical evidence of Āditya I. The reference in this inscription[9] to the grant of certain land "free of taxes to the God of the holy Mūlasthāna at Tirukkaḷukkuṉṟam"[10] by Skandaśiṣya clearly shows that a temple existed here in the 5th century A.D. Thus it is possible that this temple at Tirukkaḷukkuṉṟam must have been built of some perishable material and it must have been converted into stone later on.[11]

As for the question, where this temple existed at Tirukkaḷukkuṉṟam, we are not able to say anything certain. Scholars have put forward various suggestions in their attempt to identify the original Mūlasthāna of Skandaśiṣya association.

Firstly, it is suggested that the *Orukal maṇḍapa* represents the original Mūlasthāna referred to in Āditya I's inscription.[12] The second suggestion is that the Vedagirīśvara temple on the hill is, probably, the original Mūlasthāna.[13] The third suggestion made by S.R. Balasubramanian is that the original Mūlasthāna must have existed at the place where the Strong Room or Tiru Ābharaṇa Koṭṭadi is situated in the Bhakta-vatsala temple.[14] We shall now examine each suggestion in detail.

The reason for the first suggestion is stated to be that the Orukal Maṇḍapa is the earliest existing temple today at Tirukkaḷukkuṉṟam. But the antiquity of this cave-temple may

7. *Memoirs of Arch. Survey*, No. 17. *The Pallava Architecture,* Part I, pp. 22-23.
8. Gopinatha Rao: *Ep. Indica,* XV, p. 15.
9. 167 of 1894.
10. *Ep. Ind.*, III, p. 277.
11. N. Venkata Ramanayya: *op. cit.,* p. 63.
12. *A.R.E.* for 1909, p. 72.
13. *A.R.E.*, for 1932-33, pp. 54-55.
14. *J.M.U.*, XIV, pp. 19-21.

be taken as far back as the period of Narasimhavarman I only[15] as attested by his inscription found here. Thus it is not possible for us to identify the *Orukal Maṇḍapa* with the original Mūlasthāna that existed in the 5th century.

However, it is probable that Narasiṁhavarman I excavated the cave temple and made endowments for the original god of the Mūlasthāna, which he consecrated in the new cave temple. This view is further strengthened by the existence of an inscription of Narasiṁhavarman I which refers to "the God of Mūlasthāna on the hill".[16] That this inscription is the earliest one at this place and that it refers to the 'God of Mūlasthāna on the hill' makes us infer that there might have been in existence a temple on the hill along with the *Orukal Maṇḍapa.* But as this inscription is considered to be a renewal of the original grant made by Skandaśiṣya,[17] the original Mūlasthāna must have ceased to exist and was probably replaced by the *orukal maṇḍapa.* The original god was probably consecrated in the new cave temple, in the time of Narasiṁhavarman I.[18] Thus, it has been suggested the *Orukal Maṇḍapa.* represents the original temple.

The second suggestion is to identify the Vedagirīśvara shrine on the summit of the hill at this place, with the original Mūlasthāna, on the basis of its ancient structure,[19] and the reference to the God of Mūlasthāna on the hill, in the inscription of Narasiṁhavarman I. This is quite plausible but the difficulty is that the Vedagirīśvara shrine, as it exists today, belongs to the time of Parameśvara Varman I, as is known from the architectural features of the shrine.[20] However, we cannot set

---

15. *An. Rep. Arch. Dept. Southern Circle,* 1919-20, Part II, p.25.
16. 65 of 1909, *A.R.R.* for 1932-33, p. 55.
17. *Arch. Memoirs,* No. 17.
18. *A.R.E.* for 1932-33, pp. 54-55.
19. *A.R. Arch. Dept. Southern Circle,* 1919-20. Part II, p. 25.

---

20. *Ancient India,* XIV, p. 132. Apart from the architectural features the deity of this temple is referred to in the inscriptions of Rājādhirāja I (172 of 1894), Kulōttunga III (182 of 1894), Rājarāja III (143 of 1932-33), Kōpperuñjinga (189 A, B of 1894) & (160 of 1932-33), Māravarman Vikrama Pāṇḍya (189-C of 1894), Jaṭāvarman Sundara Pāṇḍya (59 of 1909), Bukka II (58 of 1909) and Dēva Rāya (177 of 1894) as Tirukkaḷukkuṉṟam Uḍaiya Nāyanār or

aside the possibility of the existence of a temple on the summit of the hill, which was identical with the original Mūlasthāna, before the present Vedagirīśvara shrine was reconstructed.[21] As observed by K.R. Srinivasan, "the dolmenoid structure (Vedagirīśvara Shrine) eventually replaced the brick and mortar Mūlasthāna temple of Skandaśiṣya Pallava."

The third view, put forth by Balasubramanian, is to identify the place where the Strong Room stands today, in the Bhaktavatsala temple below the hill, as the place where the original Mūlasthāna stood. He says that it is not necessary that the original Mūlasthāna should have been a rock-cut temple, as it was evidently of a brick or wooden structure of perishable nature. He also cites the example of Chidambaram where the Tirumūlasthāna was not a rock-cut one. He gives the following reasons in favour of his argument:

1. The Strong Room possesses all the features of a shrine with niches for usual deities set up in the temples of this period i.e. 9th century A.D. The room is a roofless, apsidal building in Gajapṛṣṭha style; there are sculptures of Gaṇēśa and Dakṣṇā-mūrti on the right wall (west wall); Vishṇu on the back wall (north); and Brahmā and Mahiṣāśura Mardani on the left or east wall. The room faces South. The sculptures are assigned to the 9th century A.D. as they are typical early cōḷa sculptures.

2. All the earliest grants are made to Sri Mūlasthānathu perumānaḍigaḷ from the days of Skandaśiṣya i.e. 5th century to the 14th and 15th years of Kulōttunga I (1085) a period of more than six centuries. After 1085 the name Mūlasthānathup-perumānaḍigal drops out and the god is referred to as Tirukkaḷukkuṉṟa-Uḍaiya-Nāyanār or Mahādēva. Moreover, all the earliest inscriptions are found engraved on the walls of this room.

3. The principal deity in the lower temple (Bhaktavat-salēśvara) was probably consecrated in its present form only in

---

Mahādēva on the sacred hill and all these inscriptions belong to the period after the 10th century A.D. Thus it must have replaced the original Mūlasthāna on the hill.

21. *Ancient India*, XIV, p. 132,

the 13th century.[22] This is inferred from an inscription of the 9th year of Jaṭāvarman Sundarapāṇḍya I[23] i.e. 1260 A.D. Thus, it is probable that owing to certain unknown reasons, the old Mūlasthāna i.e. the present Strong Room was given up or abandoned and the new deity was consecrated in a new shrine and old one became the strong room.

Balasubramanian concludes that the strong room had come into existence about the 9th century and it was a later structural stone temple built for the original Mūlasthāna Linga, originally consecrated perhaps in a brick structure. But this view poses a question as to why the original Mūlasthāna should have existed below the hill and not on the hill, especially where the present Vedagirīśvara shrine exists today. It is more appropriate to identify the original Mūlasthāna with the Vedagirīśvara temple on the hill. The following reasons may well support this point of view:

1. Appar and Sambandar, the two Tēvāram hymners, who lived in the beginning of the 7th century A.D., have sung in praise of the Lord of the hill called Kaḷukkuṉṟam in their hymns. Tradition also affirms that the three great Śaiva Nāyanārs, Appar, Sambandar and Sundarar, who visited this place, regarded this hill as the very embodiment of the Vēdas (Vēdagiri) and worshipped the Lord on the hill from below and this place from where they worshipped came to be known as Mūvar-Pēṭṭai. Appar, in one of his hymns, refers to the deity as "the God on the summit of the hill Kaḷukkuṉṟam."[24] It clearly shows that a temple must have existed on the hill even in the beginning of the 7th century, earlier to the Orukal Maṇḍapa.

22. The architectural features of the Bhaktavatsala shrine show beyond doubt that it must have been constructed in the early quarter of the 12th century. This is also supported by the presence of inscription dated in the 12th century, earliest of them being dated in the 47th year of Kulōttunga I i.e. 1117 A.D.
23. 188 of 1894.
24. Appar in his hymn says:
    ...காவார்ந்த பொழிற்சோலைக் கானப்பேராய்
    கழுக்குன்றத் துச்சியாய் கடவுளேநின்...

The temple must have been different from the Orukal-Maṇḍapa and in the all probability the Vedagirīśvara Temple on the hill was the Mūlasthāna shrine.

2. The inscription of Narasiṁhavarman I[25] on the Orukal-maṇḍapa refers to the "God of the Mūlasthāna on the hill" (Sriṁalaimēl). This inscription, being the earliest at this place, probably refers to the god of the original Mūlasthāna on the hill, which was consecrated in the Orukal-Maṇḍapa by Narasiṁha-varman I, after the original temple disappeared.[26]

Thus, from the foregoing discussion, it would appear that the weight of evidence lies more in favour of the Mūlasthānam having been situated on the hill rather than down below.

ORUKAL MAṆḌAPA

This is the earliest of all the temples that exist today at Tirukkaḷukkunṟam. This rock-cut temple is generally believed to have been excavated in the time of Narasiṁhavarman I, as there is an inscription of the same king on one of the pillars of the cave. But the architectural features are similar to those of the caves made during the reign of Mahendravarman I.[27] Some earlier scholars attributed it to Mahendra's time.[28] The inscription of Narasiṁhavarman I unfortunately does not tell us anything about the temple or who excavated it. It was thought by some that this cave was excavated in the reign of Mahendravarman I and this inscription, along with the figures of Brahmā and Viṣṇu, were added to it.[29] But this is not the usual practice. The latest view expressed by K.R. Srinivasan, based on his careful comparative study is to include this temple in the second group of Mahendra style, i.e., in the group of temples excavated by Narasiṁhavarman Mamalla son of Mahendravarman I.[30]

25. 65 of 1909.
26. *A.R.E.* for 1932-33, pp. 54-55 & *An. Rep. of Arch. Dept. Southern Circle,* 1919-20. Part II, p. 25.
27. *An. Rep. of Arch. Dept. Southern Circle,* 1919-20, Part II, pp. 24-26.
28. J. Dubreuil: *op. cit.,* p. 2.
29. *Memoir of Arch. Dept.,* No. 17. pp. 19-21.
30. *Ancient India,* XIV, p. 122.

The Linga that is now enshrined in this cave is said to be the original deity as suggested above, which was in worship in the Mūlasthāna of Skandaśiṣya association. Though no ceremonial worship is conducted in this temple now, the pilgrims still bow before the linga which is believed to represent Śiva, who, according to the Sthalapurāṇa, and popular tradition, cursed the two riṣis into kites that visit this place today.

VĒDAGIRĪŚVARA SHRINE ON THE HILL

The next among the extant shrines, in point of time, was that of Lord Vedagirīśvara, on the summit of the hill. This is a very ancient structure, but at first sight gives a modern appearance. It is due to later additions to the original shrine.

The main shrine is built of blocks of stone with a square sanctum, the niches on the outer wall are on the west wall, Somāskanda, Brahmā on the south, Viṣṇu on the north while in the north and south walls Yūgadakṣiṇāmūrti, and Nandikē-śvara and Chaṇḍikēśvara are carved respectively. These panels, especially that of Somāskanda on the back wall, show that this temple is architecturally later than the *Orukal Maṇḍapa*. The architectural features indicate that this temple belongs to the reign of Parameśvara Varman I.[31]

The deity of this temple is referred to as Tirukkaḻukkuṉṟam Uḍaiya-Nāyanār or Mahādēva on the sacred hill in the inscription of Rājādhirāja I,[32] Kulōttunga III,[33] Rājarāja III,[34] Kōpperuñjinga,[35] Māravarman Vikrama Pāṇḍya,[36] Jaṭā-varman Vīra Pāṇḍya Dēva I,[37] Bukka II[38] and Dēva Rāya I.[39]

31. K.R. Srinivasan, *Ancient India,* XIV, p. 132.
32. 172 of 1894.
33. 182 of 1894.
34. 143 of 1932 -33.
35. 189 A, B of 1894 and 160 of 1932-33.
36. 189-C of 1894.
37. 59 of 1909.
38. 58 of 1909.
39. 117 of 1894.

TIRU-ĀBHARAṆA-KOṬṬAḌI (THE STRONG ROOM IN THE LOWER TEMPLE)

This is the oldest part of the Bhaktavatsala Temple (down the hill) and is situated in the second Prākāra. It faces south and is a roofless semi-circular building (*Gajapṛṣṭha* style). This is a typical early Cōḷa shrine,[40] with fine niches with sculptures which show the characteristics of the 9th century A.D. Moreover, all the earliest inscriptions are found engraved on the walls of this shrine and they refer to various grants made to Sri Mūlasthānattup-perumā-naḍigaḷ, from the 27th year of Āditya I (898) to the 15th year of Kulōt-tunga I (i.e. 1085). But this name of the deity drops out from the 42nd year of Kulōt-tunga I and thereafter the deity is referred to as Tirukkaḷukkuṉṟa-muḍaiya-Nāyanār or Mahādēva. It is probably for some reason or other that this shrine must have been abandoned and a new shrine, probably the present Bhaktavatsala shrine, was consecrated and the old one became the strong room.

BHAKTAVATSALĒŚVARA SHRINE (Fig. 10)

This is the main shrine in the lower temple and is dedicated to Bhaktavatsalēśvara. The earliest inscriptions that are found on the walls of this shrine are those of Kulōttunga I (1117 A.D).[41] Many other inscriptions dated in the 12th and 13th centuries are also found on the walls of this shrine. Among them, the inscriptions of Vikrama Cōḷa (1133), Rājēndra II (1159), Rājādhirāja II (1177) of the 12th century are found. Thus, this shrine, along with the Riṣi Gōpura in front of this shrine, must have come into existence in the reign of Kulōttunga I i.e. about 1117 A.D. or a little earlier.[42] The architectural features of this shrine also attest to this fact. Moreover, the outer faces of the

40. It can also be dated earlier than the 27th year of Āditya I. See *Ancient India* XIV, p. 137 and *Ep. Ind.*, III, p. 277. See also *infra* Chap. on Architecture.
41. 124 and 137 of 1932-33.
42. There is an inscription dated in the 23rd year of Kulōttunga I i.e. 1093, on the eastern wall of the plinth of this gōpura. It is quite likely that this gōpura and the main shrine were constructed at the same time.

walls round this shrine forming the first prākāra, contain many inscriptions of the 12th century – i.e. inscription of Vikrama Cōḷa (1121-1133), Kulōttunga II (1135-1144), Rājēndra II (1159), Kulōttunga III (1198-1216) – and numerous other inscriptions of later date. All these inscriptions up to the 9th year of Jaṭāvarman Sundara Pāṇḍya I refer to the deity as Tirukkaḷukkuṉṟamuḍaiya-Nāyanār or Mahādēva. An inscription of Jaṭāvarman Sundara Pāṇḍya I's 9th year refers to the consecration of the linga of Nāyanār Poṉṉittīśvaram Uḍaiyār, by an officer of the king, Adiyamān Dēvar.[43]

MĀṆIKKAVĀCAKAR SHRINE

At the south-east corner of the second prākāra, facing west, is the small shrine dedicated to Māṇikkavācakar, who is referred to as Tirupperunturai-Āḷuḍaiyār, in the inscription found on the south wall of the shrine.[44] This inscription records an agreement made by the oil-merchants of Kāñci (modern Kāñchipuram) for the daily supply of oil for a perpetual lamp before the image of Tirupperunturai-Āḷuḍaiyār in the temple at Tirukkaḷukkuṉṟam. This shrine probably came into existence on or little before the date of this inscription, which is dated in the 3rd year of Kulōttunga II i.e. 1135 A.D. The architectural features also support its later Cōḷa date.[45] There is also another incomplete inscription of the same date beginning with the words *Pūmēvivaḷara* etc.

AVIMAṬṬĪŚVARA-MUḌAIYĀR-MAHĀDĒVA SHRINE

An inscription[46] of the 34th year of Kulōttunga III (1212) records the existence of a shrine dedicated to Avimaṭṭiśvaramuḍaiyār-Mahādēva, in the north-east corner of the temple. This inscription records a gift of cows for two perpetual lamps in this shrine by a Veḷḷāla of Kiḷkkandai in Mondūr-nāḍu, a sub-division of Āmur kōṭṭam. This inscription refers to Tirukkaḷukkuṉṟam as Śembiyan Tirukkaḷukkuṉṟam.

43. 188 of 1894. *Ind. Ant*,. XXI, p. 343.
44. 186 of 1932-33.
45. *Infra*, Chapter on Architecture.
46. 178 of 1932-33.

It is difficult to identify this shrine with any of the existing shrines at this place. It is quite likely that the shrine to the east of the Strong Room is the shrine referred to in the inscription. The architectural features of this shrine are characteristic of the later Cōḷa period.

HUNDRED-PILLARED MAṆḌAPA

Another inscription[47] of the 35th year (1213) of Kulōttunga III refers to the construction of the steps to the hundred-pillared hall in the third *prākāra* of the Bhaktavatsala temple. It is not clear whether the hundred-pillared hall was also constructed along with the steps or whether the hundred-pillared hall was already in existence and only the steps were reconstructed. The latter seems more plausible.

Another inscription[48] of the 38th year (1216) of the same king refers to the construction of a *maṇḍapa* in front of the temple. It is not clear from this record which *maṇḍapa* is referred to. But evidently, it is a reference to the *maṇḍapa* in front of the Bhaktavatsala shrine, along with the hundred-pillared hall, referred to above, in the third *prākāra*.

VINĀYAKA AND SUBRAHMAṆYA SHRINES

An inscription[49] of the 7th year (1223) of Rājarāja III records the setting up of the images of Subrahmaṇya and Vināyaka at the entrance of the temple on the hill, by Āḻuḍaiyāḷammai the wife of Śātturāyan Viraviśadan Ātchikoṇḍāṉ of Perumbachchēri in Mondūr-nādu, a subdivision of Āmur kōṭṭam. These two images must be those in the shrines at the entrance to hill. The architectural features of the shrines also testify to their later Cōḷa date.

There is no epigraphical evidence for the construction of the shrines of Utsava Vedagirīśvara, Ēkāmbaranāthar, Āthmanāthan, Vaṇduvana Piḷḷaiyār, Subrahmaṇya and Tējōlingam. But the architectural features of these shrines – the niches, the pillars and their corbels, etc., show that they belong to the later Cōḷa period.

---

47. 149 of 1932-33.
48. 144 of 1932-33.
49. 143 of 1932-33.

TIRUPURASUNDARI SHRINE

In the north-west corner of the second prākāra is the shrine of Tirpurasundari. It is a typical later Cōḷa structure with its plinth having moulded parts. The walls have well-cut niches and the pilasters have the typical later Cōḷa corbels. There are two inscriptions of the 9th year of Jaṭāvarman Sundara Pāṇḍya I (1260) on the west wall of the shrine.

MUKHA MAṆḌAPA AND ĀMAI MAṆḌAPA

We have no epigraphical records for the construction of these maṇḍapas – the Mukha-maṇḍapa in front of the Bhaktavatsala shrine and the Āmai-maṇḍapam in the south-western corner of the third prākāra. But from the point of view of architecture they may be ascribed to the Vijayanagar period,. i.e., around 16th or 17th century.

Thus, an account of the origin and growth of the temples at Tirukkaḷukkuṉṟam reveals that it was from humble beginnings that the temples at this place grew into a big temple complex. Throughout a period of well over thirteen centuries new images with shrines and new structures were introduced from time to time. In spite of these new additions at various periods, the temples at this place present an amazing unity and even make the visitor get the impression that the whole temple was constructed at one time and according to a well-integrated plan.

Chapter 5

RELIGION AND FESTIVALS

RELIGION

South India has for a long time afforded congenial ground for many religions to flourish together without sectarian bickerings. Tolerance has been the keynote of her religious atmosphere and this is well attested by the existence of temples of different faiths side by side and yet not quarrelling. Thus, within hardly nine miles flourished two great and important centres of Śaivism and Vaiṣṇavism, viz., Tirukkaḻukkuṉṟam and Mahābalipuram and there is yet no record of any clash or rivalry between the two. Mahābalipuram or Māmallai, as it was called by the Āḻvārs, was a holy place for the Vaiṣṇavas. The Sthalaśayana Perumāl temple at this place has been sung by Būdattāḻvar[1] and Tirumangai Āḻvar.[2] This place was the birth-place of the former. Narasiṁhavarman I Māmalla who beautified Mamallapuram with his splendid architectural activity, which included shrines for Viṣṇu (like the two Varaha caves). But the same king also excavated the *orukal maṇḍapa* at Tirukkaḻukkuṉṟam, dedicated to Śiva and showed that he was a king with liberal outlook, who rose above all narrow sectarian bias.

---

1. K.A.N. Sastri: *History of South India*, p. 408. The three early Aḻvars, of whom Būdattāḻvār is one, are assigned to a date not later than the fifth and sixth centuries A.D.
2. Tirumangai is assigned to the middle of the 8th century A.D.

The iconographic representation inside the cave at Tirukkaḻukkuṉṟam also attests to the fact that during the Pallava days Śiva and Viṣṇu images had not got isolated into watertight compartments but actually the shrines and the sculptures of Viṣṇu and Śiva are found side by side in many places. The early Āḻvārs prior to Tirumangai (8th century) sing in their hymns about the inseparable nature of Viṣṇu and Śiva godheads.[3] And we find this attitude well translated into sculptural form at Tirukkaḻukkuṉṟam. Inside the *Orukal Maṇḍapa* are the bold sculptural representations of Trimūrti-Śiva, Viṣṇu and Brahmā, thus showing that the religious atmosphere was one of cordiality, especially between the Śaiva and Vaiṣṇava faiths.

During the Pallava period, when the whole of the Tamil country was in the grip of a great Bhakti movement fostered by the Vaiṣṇava Āḻvārs and Śaiva Nāyanmārs, Tirukkaḻukkuṉṟam attracted the eminent *Tēvāram* trio who visited this place and sang in honour of the presiding Lord there, in great ecstasy. Later still, about the 9th century A.D. Māṇikkavācakar, the great Śaiva saint, visited and sang about the place. In the 10th century Paṭṭinattu Aḍigaḷ and in the 15th century Aruṇagirināthar also visited and sang in praise of the Lord and the place. Thus, the visits of these celebrities undoubtedly constitute prominent landmarks in the history of Śaivism at Tirukkaḻukkuṉṟam.

APPAR

Appar or Tirunāvukkaraśar was the first of the Dēvāram trio to visit Tirukkaḻukkuṉṟam. He was a veḷḷāḷa from Tiruvāmūr in the South Arcot district and lived in the beginning of the 7th century A.D. In his early days he was much attracted to Jainism and took to that religion. But he was brought back to Śaivism by the efforts of his sister. After he became a Śaiva he undertook pilgrimage to all the holy Śaiva temples in the Tamil country, with a determination to spread the Śaiva religion. In the course of his pilgrimage, he visited Tirukkaḻukkuṉṟam

3. *J.I.H.*, Vol. XXXI, part I (Dec. 1953), p. 250.

and worshipped and sang a *padigam* in praise of the Lord of Kaḻukkuṉṟam (only three verses are available now). That Appar was very much attracted by the Lord of Kaḻukkuṉṟam is evident from his hymns where he expresses great pleasure in having worshipped Him. He says at the end of the verse one,

காவலனைக் கழுக்குன்றம் அமர்ந்தான் தன்னைக்
கற்பகத்தைக் கண்ணாரக் கண்டேன் நானே[4]

and in verse two,

கல்லாடை புனைந்தருளுங் கபாலியைக்
கற்பகத்தைக் கண்ணாரக் கண்டேன் நானே[5]

In the third verse, he had all praise for the Lord of the place and he says,

தேவார்ந்த தேவனைத் தேவரெல்லாம்
திருவடிமேல் அலரிட்டுத் தேடி நின்று
நாவார்ந்த மறைபாடி நட்டம் ஆடி
நான்முகனும் இந்திரனும் மாலும் போற்றக்
காவார்ந்த பொழிற்சோலைக் கானப்பேராய்
கழுக்குன்றத் துச்சியாய் கடவுளே நின்
பூவார்ந்த பொன்னடிக்கே போதுகின்றேன்
பூம் புகலூர் மேவிய புண்ணியனே[6]

SAMBANDAR

Sambandar or Tiruñānasambandar, another *Tēvāram* hymner hailed from Siyali in the Tanjavur district. He was a younger contemporary of Appar and, like the latter, undertook a tour of pilgrimage to all the important temples of Tamilnad, in order to spread the tenets of Śaivism and stamp out the influence of non-vedic religions. In the course of his visit to holy shrines, he visited Tirukkaḻukkuṉṟam and sang a *padigam* on the Lord of Kaḻukkuṉṟam.[7]

---

4. *Appar Tēvāram*: Tirukkaḻukkuṉṟap-padigam, verse 1.
5. *Ibid.*, verse 2.
6. *Ibid.*, verse 3.
7. கண்ணார் **கழுக்குன்றம்** கயிலை கோணம்
பயில் கற்குடி காளத்தி வாட்போக்கியும்
பண்ணார் மொழி மங்கையோர் பங்குடையான்
பரங்குன்றம் பருப்பதம்
(R.P. Sethu Pillai: *Urum Pērum*, p. 173). Sambandar himself refers in the hymn to the holy places he visited.

The way in which he expressed his happiness in having worshipped the Lord of this place at the end of every verse of his *padigam,* shows his great devotion to the temple.

In one of his verses on Tirukkaḷukkuṉṟam, he praises the Lord as one who had vanquished the Buddhists and Jains.[8] It shows that he was such a staunch opponent of Buddhism and Jainism that he condemned them almost in every one of his hymns.

SUNDARAR

Sundaramūrti Nāyaṉār, another *Tēvāram* hymner, came a century later than Appar and Sambandar. He was born of a poor Brahmin family in Nāvalūr in South Arcot district. He was turned to a life of religion and piety by the mysterious intervention of Śiva, while he was about to marry a girl. Thereupon, he undertook a tour of pilgrimage to the important Śaiva centres in the Tamil country. He visited Tirukkaḷukkuṉṟam in the course of his tour, and sang a *padigam* on the Lord of the place. That he was much attracted by the god is well brought out by his verses in which he appeals to the people to go to Kaḷukkuṉṟam and worship the Lord there. He says, for example:

சென்று சென்று தொழுமின் தேவர் பிரானிடம்[9]
இறங்கிச் சென்று தொழுமின் இன்னிசை பாடியே[10]
நீளநின்று தொழுமின் நித்தலும் நீதியால்
ஆளும் நம் வினைகள் அல்கி அழிந்திட ...[11]
புலைகள் தீர தொழுமின் புன்சடைப் புண்ணியன்[12]
வெளிறு தீரத் தொழுமின் வெண் பொடியாடியை[13]

MĀṆIKKAVĀCAKAR

About the middle of the 9th century A.D.[14] came Māṇikkavācakar, who was first a minister of a Pāṇḍyan ruler Varaguṇa.

8. Verse 10:
   சாய நின்றான் வன்சமண் குண்டர் சாக்கியர்
9. *Sundarar Tēvāram*; Tirukkaḷukkuṉṟap-padigam, verse 1.
10. *Ibid.,* verse 2.
11. *Ibid.,* verse 3.
12. *Ibid.,* verse 5.
13. *Ibid.,* verse 4.
14. He was a contemporary of Varaguṇa Pāṇḍya II; see Sastri, K.A.N. *A History of South India.*

He was a staunch opponent of Buddhism and Jainism, and is said to have vanquished them in arguments.[15] His hymns are collected together in the *Tiruvācakam*. He played an important role in the Hindu revivalism in the Pāṇḍyan country. Though his life is intimately connected with the temple at Chidambaram, he visited many centres of Śaivism among which Tirukkaḷukkuṉṟam is very important.

He has also sung a *padigam* in honour of the Lord of this place with great ecstasy. According to tradition, he had the *darśan* of Lord Śiva at Kaḷukkuṉṟam in the same form as at Tirupperunturai. He refers to this in all the verses of his *padigam*. To cite a few examples, he says:

பிணக்கிலா பெருந்துறைப் பெரு
  மானுன் னாமங்கள் பேசுவார்க்கு
கணக்கிலாத்திருக் கோலம் நீவந்து
  காட்டினாய் கழுக்குன்றிலே[16]
பேதமில்லா தார் கற்பளித்த
  பெருந்துறைப் பெருவள்ளமே
காதலாலுனை யோத நீ வந்து
  காட்டினாய் கழுக்குன்றிலே[17]

That the memory of the association of these devotees was kept alive in subsequent days is attested by the fact that there arose popular legends connected with their visit to this place. The place, where there is a small *maṇḍapa*, to the east of the hill, Vedagiri, is believed to be the place from where the Nāyanmārs worshipped the deity on the hill. It is believed that the Nāyanmārs did not set their foot on the hill as they considered it to be the very embodiment of the Vedas. This place has come to be known as *Mūvar Peṭṭai*[18] and the maṇḍapa as Nālvar kōil, adding Māṇikkavācakar to the above three. There is also a legend connected with Sundarar, who prayed for and received gold from the Lord.[19]

15. *Ibid*
16. R. Visvanathaier: *Tiruvāsaga Vyākyanam*, Part II, pp. 814 to 819 (Madras Government Oriental Series: No. CXIII), verse 66.
17. *Ibid.*, verse 471.
18. *J.M.U.*, XIV, pp. 20-22.
19. See Chapter 2.

An inscription in the temple at this place shows that as early as the 3rd year of Kulōttunga II (1135 A.D.) there was a shrine dedicated to Māṇikkavācakar within the Bhaktavatsala temple. This refers to him as Tirupperunturai Āluḍaiyār and records an agreement made by the oil-merchants of Kāñci to supply oil for a perpetual lamp in this shrine.[20]

PAṬṬINATTU AḌIGAḶ

The visit of Paṭṭinattu Adigaḷ is another landmark in the history of Śaivism at Tirukkaḻukkuṉṟam. He lived about the 10th century A.D.[21] He was born in Kāverippūmpaṭṭinam and was leading a happy and contented life. But suddenly he realised the uselessness of life in this unreal world and renounced everything and became an ascetic. He became a devotee of Śiva and visited the holy places. He came to Tirukkaḻukkuṉṟam and sang in praise of Śiva and the place.

ARUṆAGIRINĀTHAR

Aruṇagirināthar, whose songs are collected into the *Tiruppugaḻ*, was another Śaiva saint associated with this place. He lived in the 15th century A.D. He was born in Tiruvaṇṇāmalai in the North Arcot district and in his early days he led a life full of vices. But after some time he realised the folly and wanted to put an end to his life by jumping down from the top of the *gōpura* of the temple at Tiruvaṇṇāmalai. But he was saved by Śiva himself. From then on he dedicated his life to the cause of spreading Śaivism in the Tamil country and became a true devotee of Muruga. He also visited all the important centres of Śaivism including Tirukkaḻukkuṉṟam and composed beautiful verses on Lord Muruga. There are four verses on Tirukkaḻukkuṉṟam in his *Tiruppugaḻ* of which the verse beginning with

ஓலமிட்ட சுரும்பு தனா தனாவென
வேசிரத்தில் விழுங்கை பளீர் பளீரென
வோசை பெற்ற சிலம்பு கலீர் கலீரென [22]

20. Chapter 4.
21. Anavaradavinayagam Pillai: *Tamil Perumakkal Varalāru*, pp. 192-94.
22. *Tiruppugal*-verse 320 (*Tiruppugal* edited by M.R. Kandasami Kavirayar; published by E.M. Gopalakrishna Konar (1955)).

is the most popular among the people. In one of his verses he refers to Tirukkaḷukkuṉṟam as கழுகுதொழு வேதகிரி[23] (the hill worshipped by kites) and in another as வேதவெற்பு (hill of Vedas).[24]

After the 15th century many poets and scholars composed devotional songs on the Lord of this place. Among them mention may be made of Chidambarasvamigal of Tiruppōrur who has sung a *padigam* on Vedagirīśvara, Viraraghava Mudaliar,[25] the author of the Tamil *Sthalapurāṇa* and *Tirukkaḷukkuṉṟa Ulā* and Kanniappa Mudaliyar, who sang the *Mahālingap-padigam* on *Vedagirīśvara*. There are other works like *Tirukkaḷukkuṉṟa-Mālai, Tirukkaḷukkuṉṟa Ślēdai Veṇba*.

Thus it is clear from the above account that Tirukkaḷuk-kuṉṟam was a very popular and holy centre of Śaivism and that it had attracted important Śaiva celebrities, through the ages.

MAṬHAS

Apart from the visits of great devotees, the existence of some maṭhas at this place also facilitated the growth of Śaivism. There was a *maṭha* named after Naminanda Aḍigaḷ, one of the 63 Śaiva devotees, whose lives are recapitulated in the *Peria Purāṇam*, a work of the 12th century. An inscription of Kulōttunga I records the grant of some land, purchased from the inhabitants of Vānavan-Mādēvi-Caturvēdimangalam, by the temple authorities, for 10 *kāśu* given to them by a resident of Rājarājapuram.[26] There was another *maṭha* at this place in the reign of Kulōttunga III to which a house-site was sold by a *Mahēśvara* of Vaipākkam in Mōndūr-nāḍu, a sub-division of Śembūr-kōṭṭam. The *maṭha* was probably presided over by Śivadavanapperumāḷ Agōradēva-Rāvalar, mentioned in the

23. *Ibid.*, verse 321; R.P. Sethu Pillai: *Ūrum Pērum, p.* 173.
24. *Ibid.*, verse 320.
25. Viraraghava Mudaliyar was a learned Tamil poet who lived in the 18th century A.D. An account of his life is given by U.V. Swaminathaier in *Tirukkaḷukkuṉṟa Ulā*, pp. 20-22.
26. 179 of 1894; *S.I.I*, III, No. 75 & *I.A*,. XXI, p. 284.

inscription.[27] The importance of these maṭhas and their activities cannot be exaggerated and they must have played some part in spreading Śaivism among the local people.

Thus the ancient character of this place and its association with the greatest of the Nāyanmārs and other great religious apostles, must have made Tirukkaḷukkuṉṟam a popular centre of Śaivism. As such, it attracted the patronage of many chiefs and royal officers, from very early times, who lavished gifts as tokens of their devotion to the temples at this place.

FESTIVALS

Hindu temples are noted for their innumerable festivals and religious ceremonies which take place round the year. In ancient days the temple was the centre of attraction in the social and religious life of the people and festivals were conducted frequently by the joint endeavour and enthusiasm of the people. Festivals, though essentially religious ceremonies, afforded opportunities for the relatives and friends to meet, exchange views, settle marriages etc. So, the celebration of festivals in a village was a fair indication of the religions fervour and social dynamism of the people. At Tirukkaḷukkuṉṟam a number of festivals are conducted even today in different months of the year and they attract large crowds even from distant parts.

Throughout the year a number of festivals are celebrated in the temples at Tirukkaḷukkuṉṟam. Of these, three are important ones celebrated for Lord Vedagirīśvara.[28] They are: 1. *Brahmōtsava* or *Mahōtsava* in the month of *Cittirai*; 2. Abhiṣeka with 1008 *Sankus* in the month of *Kārttikai* and 3. *Teppa Utsava* or the Floating Festival in the month of *Tai*. In the Bhaktavatsala temple important festivals are performed to Goddess Tirupurasundari in the months of *Āḍi*, *Puraṭṭāsi* and *Panguni*. The most important is the *Navarātri* (Nine nights) festival in *Puraṭṭāsi*. There are a number of annual festivals conducted for other deities like Vināyaka and Subrahmaṇya and the Nāyanmārs. We shall now describe the festivals in detail.

---

27. 145 of 1932-33.
28. These festivals are conducted to the *Utsava* image of Vedagirīśvara which is enshrined in a shrine in the Bhaktavatsala temple.

BRAHMŌTSAVA IN THE VEDAGIRĪŚVARA TEMPLE

Brahmōtśava or Mahōtsava, the annual festival, is the most spectacular one and is celebrated for ten days in the month of *Cittirai* (April-May). This festival commences with *Dhvaja rōhaṇa* which falls on the *Mrigasirṣa Nakṣatra*. In all the ten days the deity is taken in procession through the streets of the village, both in the morning and evening. The festivals on the third, fourth, fifth and seventh days are of special importance and are conducted in a grand manner.

On the third day early in the morning, Vedagirīśvara is seated on the bull, *Adikāra* Nandi and taken in procession round the outer *prākāra* and then to the north *gōpura*, where a festival takes place. This is probably to commemorate the traditional account of Nandi doing penance here, near the Nandi Tank and having his sin redeemed by Lord Śiva. This festival attracts a large number of devotees. In the evening Vedagirīśvara is taken in a grand procession round the hill, Vedagiri, accompanied by the 63 Nāyanārs. The procession covers a distance of two and a half miles.

The festival on the fourth day is to keep alive the memory of the visit of Sundaramūrti Nāyanār to this place. On this day Vedagirīśvara is seated on the serpent vehicle (Nāga Vāhana) and is taken in procession through the Western entrance (gōpura) to a *maṇḍapa*, known as *Kaṇakkar Maṇḍapa*, situated in the southwest corner of the village. This is probably to signify that Vedagirīśvara goes in secret to hide himself from Sundaramūrti Nāyanār to whom He had promised to give some gold. Hence this procession is not accompanied by any instrumental music. Then the image of Sundaramūrti Nāyanār seated on the *Vāhana* of elephant, is taken out of the temple through the southern *gōpura* to the same *maṇḍapa*, as if he goes in search of Lord Vedagirīśvara where he receives gold from Him.[29]

On the fifth day morning, the deity is taken in procession on a *vāhana* decorated like a plantain tree (*kadali*) which is the

29. *Tirukkalukkunra Ulā* edited by Swaminathaier, p. 12. On this account the deity is also known as Poṉṉittisvarar.

sacred tree (Sthala Vṛkṣa) of the place.[30] In the night the deity is seated on *Riṣabavāhana* of silver. This festival is celebrated in a grand manner and attracts the largest crowd and people from far and near assemble here to have *darśan* of the God, who is represented as granting boons to the devotees.

The *Rathotsava* (car festival) that takes place on the seventh day is the most attractive of all the festivals. Early in the morning the deity is seated in the chariot (*tēr*) and is taken in procession round the temple.

The annual festivals come to an end on the eleventh day with the ceremony of *Ṭīrthavāri* i.e. the sacred bath to the deity at about noon. The deity is taken in procession from the temple to the *Sankutīrtham* tank where the ceremony takes place. After this ceremony, the deity is taken in procession round the hill, Vedagiri, before it is taken back to the temple.

ABHIṢEKA WITH 1008 SANKUS

On the last Monday in the month of *Kārttikai* (October-November) every year, a grand festival of sacred bath takes place on the hill to Vedagirīśvara. This *abhiṣeka* is performed with 1008 Sankus (conches) as vessels, of which some are taken out of the Sankutīrtham tank. This ceremony takes place probably to commemorate the visit of Mārkaṇḍēya to this place.[31]

KĀRTTIKAI DĪPAM

In the night of the full-moon day in the same month *Kārttikai, Kārttikai Dīpam,* a festival of lights, takes place. The whole village, including the hill, Vedagiri, and the temples, is illuminated with gentle glimmer of oil lamps which makes the village a fairyland of lights. There is also a procession of Vedagirīśvara through the illuminated streets. There is also the celebration of *Cokkappānai* in which a tall stem of tree is planted on the ground in front of the temple and dry leaves and

---

30. The place is hence known as Kadalivanam (plantain grove) கதலிவனமேவு பெருமாளே (Tiruppugaḻ).

31. See Chapter 2.

twigs are collected around the stem and set on fire. The burning of the tree provides an enjoyable sight.

According to the tradition Śiva is said to have destroyed the aerial chariots of some *asuras* who were harassing the sages and other devotees. The *Cokkappānai* symbolises the aerial chariots of the *asuras* which are burnt by the fire from Śiva's third eye.

However, the festival of *Kārttikai Dīpam* is a propitiation of *Agni* or Fire. Thus the temples as well as the houses are illuminated throughout the month of *Kārttikai* in general and on the *Śiva Kārttikai* night in particular.

PARIVĒṬṬAI

The festival of *Parivēṭṭai* represents Vedagirīśvara going to a hill for hunting wild beasts. This festival takes place on the third day of the month of *Tai* (Jan.-Feb.). Early in the morning the deity is taken in procession to the hill at Kīraip pākkam[32] a village near Tirukkaḷukkuṉṟam and the whole day is spent on the hill. A festival takes place there and in the evening the deity returns to Tirukkaḷukkuṉṟam.

TEPPA UTSAVA

The *Teppa* or Float festival is conducted every year on the *Puṣya Nakṣatra* in the month of *Tai* (*Tai Pūśam*). On this occasion a wooden pavilion (*maṇḍapa*) decorated with flowers and lights is floated in the water of the *Sankutīrtham* tank and the deity is seated in it. The *maṇḍapa* is gently pulled, with the help of ropes tied to it, round the tank several times.

It is a colourful festival and the people throng the banks of the tank in thousands to witness and worship the Lord.

There is a traditional account attached to the origin of the festival, *Tai Pūśam*. It is said that Pārvati bestowed on Subrahmaṇya a weapon called *Vēlāyudha* on the day of *Tai Pūśam*.

On the next day another *Teppa Utsava* takes place in the *Nanditīrtham* tank inside the Bhaktavatsala temple. This is also conducted with great eclat.

---

32. The earliest mention of this village is made in an inscription of the 42nd year of Kulōttunga I (1112 A.D.), 179 of 1894; *S.I.I.*, III, No. 75.

A reference is probably made to these two festivals in an inscription of Vīra Vijaya Bhūpatirāya (about 1408 A.D.)[33] of the Vijayanagar dynasty. The record says that in order to meet the expenses of the *Tai* festival (probably *Teppa*) and procession (*Parivēṭṭai*) of the deity, the merchant communities of this place agreed to pay certain amount of money collected as tax on their merchandise, to the temple treasury.[34] The agent of the king who collected the tax was one Nagēśvaramuḍaiyan Villavarayan. This shows that these festivals are conducted in the temple from a very long time.

FESTIVALS FOR TIRUPURASUNDARI

ĀḌIPPŪRAM (JULY-AUGUST)

A ten-day festival takes place for Goddess Tirupurasundari in the month of Āḍi. This is known as *Āḍippūram* festival and it starts with the *Baraṇi Nakṣatra* and ends with the *Pūram Nakṣatra*. The significance of this festival is to propitiate the Goddess Śakti or Pārvati who is considered to have come into this world on this occasion to bless the people. Therefore devotees worship her to secure happiness for themselves and the villages as a whole. If *Āḍippūram* falls on a Friday, it is considered to be highlymeritorious.

There is an inscription at Tirukkaḻukkuṉṟam recording a festival by name *Kālingarāyan-Śandi*, observed on the *Pūrvāsada nakṣatra* in the month of *Aṛpasi*. This festival is said to have been instituted by one *Kālingarāyan* of Kappalūr or Ulagaḷanda Śōḻa nallūr in Mattūṟṟukkūrram, a sub-division of Pāṇḍimaṇḍalam, probably after his name.[35] To meet the expenses of this festival a tax-free gift of a village called Karumā-rappākkam was made to the temple by assembly of Kaḷattūr*paṟṟu*. This record is dated in the 13th year of Jaṭāvarman Vīra Pāṇḍya (i.e. 1323 A.D.).[36] This shows that this festival is in observance for a

33. *A.R.E.* for 1909, p. 114.
34. 63 of 1909; *South Indian Temple Inscriptions,* Vol. I, p. 464.
35. 59 of 1909; *S.I.T.I.,* Vol. I, No. 474. His benefactions to the temples of Kanchi are also known to us from inscriptions. See K.V. Raman: *Sri Varadarajaswami Temple, Kanchi.*
36. *A.R.E.* for 1909, p. 81 (59 of 1909).

long time and the observance of *Āḍippūram* in *Aṛpasi* is said to be rather unique. But today this festival is conducted only in the month of *Āḍi.*

On the last day of this festival a grand ceremony of *Sarvānga Abhiṣeka* (to bathe the whole body of the image) to the *Mūlasthāna* deity is conducted. This *abhiṣeka* is performed only thrice a year. The other two occasions on which this ceremony is performed are: 1. On the ninth day of *Navarātri* in the month of *Puraṭṭāsi* and 2. On the *Uttira Nakṣatram* in the month of *Panguni*. Only *pādapūja* (to bathe the feet only) is performed to the Goddess every day.

NAVARĀTRI FESTIVAL

Every year in the month of *Puraṭṭāsi* (Sept.-Oct.) a magnificent festival of nine nights, popularly known as Navarātri, is celebrated in the shrine of Tirupurasundari. This festival commences on the first day in the bright fortnight of the month *Puraṭṭāsi*. All these nights Tirupurasundari is dressed in various aspects of Kāḷi e.g. Durgā, Umā, Mahiṣasuramardani, etc. This festival is performed with great pomp and piety and it attracts a large number of devotees, especially women.

On the last day of this festival, a holy bath (*Sarvānga abhiṣeka*) is performed to Her, for the second time in a year. The *Navarātri* festival is conducted within the precincts of the temple.

The significance of *Navarātri* is probably to propitiate the Goddess, who is the symbol of every kind of energy in the world, in order to obtain perpetual happiness and prosperity.

PANGUNI UTTIRAM

The *Panguni Uttiram* festival takes place on the *Uttira Nakṣatra* in the month of *Panguni* (March-April). On this occasion, *Sarvānga* is performed to Tirupurasundari, for the third time in a year. A ceremony of *Tirukkalyanam* sacred marriage is performed to Tirupurasundari. A procession of the *Utsava* deity on the *Nandi Vāhana* takes place. It is generally believed that on this day the Goddess is said to have married

Lord Śiva and to observe this festival on this particular day is to receive the blessings of the Goddess.

FESTIVALS CONNECTED WITH OTHER SHRINES IN THE BHAKTAVATSALA TEMPLE

VAṆḌUVANA PIḶḶAIYĀR

In the month of *Āvani* (August-September) an important festival is conducted to Pillaiyār or Gaṇeśa. This is known as *Vināyaka Caturti*. It falls on the fourth day in the bright fortnight of the month *Āvani*. Vināyaka is generally considered to be the remover of obstacles and the significance of celebrating this festival is to obtain knowledge and success in all undertakings. On this day the *utsavamūrti* of the deity is seated on his mount *mūṣaka* or rat, and taken in procession through the streets of the village.

MĀṆIKKAVĀCAKAR

Festivals are conducted for Māṇikkavācakar in the month of *Āṇi* and *Mārgaḷi* and the festivals in the latter month are more important. A ten-day festival takes place for him in *Mārgaḷi.*

NAṬARĀJA

In the month of *Āṇi* on the *Uttira Nakṣatra* a holy bath is performed to Naṭarāja. During the night of the same day, the deity is taken in procession. Similar festival is performed to Naṭarāja in the month of *Mārgaḷi.*

SUBRAHMAṆYA

The festival of *Mahā Skanda Ṣaṣṭi* takes place for 6 days in the bright fortnight of the month of *Aṛpasi* (October-November). This festival is observed mainly to propitiate Lord Subrahmaṇya, son of Śiva, for having destroyed the *asura*, Sūrapadma. On all these six days *abhiṣeka* is performed to Subrahmaṇya. On the last day he is taken in procession on his *Vāhana*, peacock. On these occasions *Tiruppugaḷ* verses are recited with great devotion.

SANKUTĪRTHA LAKṢADĪPAM

Apart from the annual festivals, a festival of *Lakṣadīpam* takes place once in twelve years. This is a spectacular one and is celebrated on the day when a *Sanku* or conch appears in the *Sankutīrtham* tank. This festival is probably to commemorate the visit of Mārkaṇḍēya to this place. When Mārkaṇḍēya visited this place he had no vessel to perform *abhiṣeka* to Lord Śiva. He prayed to Him and a conch appeared in the tank with which he performed the *abhiṣeka.*

This festival is celebrated when *Guru* joins *Kaṉya Rāśi.* Special *Pūjās* and *Yāgās* are performed as specified by the Āgamās for five days before this. On the day when *Guru* joins *Kaṉya Rāśi* a conch appears in the tank. The waters of the holy rivers all over the country are said to be present in this tank and a bath on this occasion is considered to be very holy[37] and effective as to eradicate the sin and consequently devotees throng here to take bath in the sacred tank. A festival takes place to Vedagirīśvara near the tank.

At night a festival of lights takes place and about a lakh of oil lamps are lit all over the hill and the temples.

We have references in inscriptions to some of the festivals that were celebrated in the temple in ancient days. An inscription of the 47th year of Kulōttunga I records the provision to supply a thousand *Nāḷi* of cow's ghee for the sacred bath of the deity on the day of *Tiruvādirai* in the month of *Mārgaḷi.*[38]

Another inscription of the 18th year of Rājarāja III refers to an *abhiṣeka* called as *Ānañju* bath i.e. bath with five products of the cow. For this a gift of eight cows was made to thc temple by a resident of Kaḷattūr.[39] Yet another inscription of Bukka II's time (1404-06)[40] records a festival called *Bukkarāyan-Śandi*

37. This is similar to one at Kumbakonam where Mahāmaka festival is celebrated.
38. 137 of 1932-33.
39. 164 of 1932-33. In all probability this bath was conducted daily as it is said in the inscription that a gift of eight cows was made for the daily supply of ghee, curd, cowdung etc.
40. *J.M.U.,* XIV, p. 21. Appendix.

which was probably named after and instituted by Bukka II. The inscription records the gift of a tax-free village to the temple[41] of Tirukkaḷukkuṉṟa-muḍaiya Nāyaṉār. Nothing is said about the occasions on which these festivals are conducted.

Thus, from the foregoing chapter it can be gathered that Tirukkaḷukkuṉṟam was an important centre of Śaivism and that many great Śaiva saints have visited and sung about the place. There were monasteries or *maṭhas* to propagate the religious tenets. People showed their reverence to God by celebrating a number of festivals to the different deities of the temple. These festivals must have also served as grand social gatherings for the people to meet and discuss common problems and witness cultural performances like music and dance.

41. 57 of 1909; *S.I.T.I.*, Vol. I, pp. 461-62.

Chapter 6

TEMPLE, ECONOMY AND SOCIETY

A study of the administration, social and economic life of the place and its people is as important as the study of political history. To know the customs and habits of the people and the social and economic conditions that prevailed therein, the inscriptions found at Tirukkaḷukkuṉṟam are of the greatest help, though they do not furnish us a complete picture. The social and economic aspects of the people's life were, to a great extent, influenced by the activities of the temples at this place.

ADMINISTRATION OF THE VILLAGE AND THE TEMPLES

From early times South India was divided into many territorial divisions for administrative purposes. The largest division was the *maṇḍala* equivalent to the modern State. The *maṇḍala* was divided into several *kōṭṭams* (districts) which were sub-divided into many *nāḍus* (taluks). Tirukkaḷukkuṉṟam, throughout the ages, formed part of Kaḷattūr nāḍu in the Kaḷattūr kōṭṭam in Toṇḍaimaṇḍalam later known as Jayangoṇḍasōḷa-maṇḍalam, except for a short time during the reign of Rājādhirāja I. During this reign Tirukkaḷukkuṉṟam is said to have formed part of Kaḷattūr nāḍu in the Adirājarāja-Kōṭṭam.[1] This was probably a mere change of the name of the old division, for, we find in the inscriptions of Rājēndra II the old name revived.[2]

1. *S.I.I.*, V, No. 465 (172 of 1894).
2. *Ibid.*, No. 466 (173 of 189).

The villages formed the lowest units of the administrative structure in South India. The administration of the village was carried out by the village assembly or *Sabhā*. These assemblies enjoyed considerable autonomy in discharging their duties of which the most important was to take care of the welfare of the people of the village and to safeguard their interests.

The earliest reference to the existence of the *Sabhā* at Tirukkaḷukkuṉṟam is made in the inscription of Parāntaka I.[3] Several inscriptions, from the time of Parāntaka I to that of the Vijayanagar kings, mention the functioning of the *Sabhā*. The *Sabhā* at Tirukkaḷukkuṉṟam probably included as its members those residents of the village who possessed high qualifications by virtue of their learning, age and property. The members were variously referred to as Mahēśvaras,[4] Ūravar and Nagarattār.[5]

POWERS OF THE SABHĀ

Though the duties of the *Sabhā* were wide and varied, one of its main functions related to the management of temple affairs. Thus the *Sabhā* acted as the trustee of the charitable endowments made to the temple, from time to time, by various rulers, royal chiefs and officials. That almost all the gifts to the temples at this place were deposited with the *Sabhā* is well brought out by the inscriptions.[6] The *Sabhā* received gifts of various kinds viz. gold,[7] cow,[8] sheep,[9] pieces of lands[10] etc. on behalf of the temple. The lands thus given as gifts to the temple were probably known by the name Tirunāmattukkāṇi.[11] It also purchased lands from private individuals and *Sabhās* of other villages, for conducting certain services in the temple.[12] It was also in its

---

3. 168 of 1894; *S.I.I*, III, p. 280.
4. *S.I.I.*, III, No. 69.
5. 172 of 1894; *S.I.I.*, V, No. 465.
6. E.G. 168, 169, 171, 172 of 1894; *S.I.I.*, V, Nos. 461, 462, 464, 465.
7. 122, 185 of 1932-33.
8. 127, 146, 151, 177, 184 etc. of 1932-33.
9. 150, 157, 165, 183 etc. of 1932-33.
10. 121, 131, 174, 176, etc. of 1932-33.
11. 147, 174 of 1932-33.
12. 179 of 1894; *I.A.*, XXI, p. 284 & 133, 154, 155, 156 etc. of 1932-33.

sphere of authority to sell the temple lands or properties to private individuals in order to carry out certain repairs in the temple with the proceeds of the sold properties.[13]

But there were instances where certain gifts were entrusted to the *Śivabrāhmaṇas* of the temple. An inscription records an agreement made by a *Śivabrāhmaṇa* of the temple to burn a lamp in the temple for the cows received from a person called Kunran, to whose father the cows were previously entrusted by people for the same purpose.[14] Another inscription also records an endowment of money for a lamp being entrusted to the *Śivabrāhmaṇa* of the temple.[15] The *Śivabrāhmaṇas*, in all probability, included the *arcakas* of the temples who enjoyed an honoured position among the people.

LAW AND ORDER

The *Śabhā* also discharged certain other duties which were in the interest of both the village and the temple. The important among them was the maintenance of law and order. It is of great interest to note that a regular system of maintaining watchmen to look after the security of the villages and temples was in prevalence in South India from early times. An inscription at Tirukkaḷukkuṉṟam refers to a grant of land known as *Kāval-kāṇi* to a person for guarding the village and the temple. It seems that the *Śabhā* set apart a piece of land of the temple as *Kāval-kāṇi* to be utilised by the watchman as remuneration for his services to the people. Unfortunately, the date of this inscription is lost.

JUSTICE

Among the numerous activities of the village *Sabhā* the maintenance of justice appears to have been prominent. There are instances where the village *Sabhā* or assembly was allowed to try criminal cases.[16] An inscription at Tirukkaḷukkuṉṟam gives us some insight into the administration of justice that

13. 188 of 1894 & 144, 169 of 1932-33.
14. 153 of 1932-33.
15. 135 of 1932-33.
16. T.V. Mahalingam: *South Indian Polity*, p. 235.

prevailed in those days. The inscription dated in the sixth year of Kulōttunga II refers to a case of murder. One Vikramādittan Kamban, a military officer of Śambuvarāya, had killed another officer, Rāman Ambalakkūttan or Tennāttaraiyan of Malaiyanūr in Panaiyūr-nāḍu, a sub-division of Milāḍu, also known as Irungoḷapāḍi. The latter's wife, Vēmbu, also died with her husband committing *sati*. This case was tried by the *Sabhā* and at the instance of Śambuvarāya and the elders of the *nāḍu*, the criminal was asked to provide the temple with some cows and sheep for two perpetual lamps in the temple. Though it was a case of wanton murder which merited much more severe punishment we do not come across instances of greater punishment for such acts of homicide.[17]

Another inscription of the 12th year of Kulōttunga II also records an interesting case. Two persons, Eḷuvān Vañji Muttaraiyan and Nakkamb-pattala Iḷavaraiyan or Śelvan, went together for hunting. The former killed the latter accidentally with an arrow and the case came before the *Sabhā*. It was decided in the usual expiation for such unintended crime. The person who committed the crime was asked to provide for a perpetual lamp in the temple for the merit of the deceased.[18] There is also another instance where a gift of sheep was made to the temple to provide a half-lamp by an individual in expiation for some injury done to another individual.[19] This inscription is dated in the 12th year of Rājarāja III.

Cases connected with the temples also came before the *Sabhā*. An inscription at this place records that one Āittān had stolen 150 *poṉ* from the gold garland of a deity, by breaking open the room where the garland was kept and plastered the opening with mortar. The *Maikāval* lodged a complaint to the trustees of the temple. When the case came for hearing before the assembly.. Āittān had run away from the village and hence his properties and the special rights enjoyed by him in the temple were sold in public auction for 850 *poṉ* and credited to the temple treasury.[20]

17. 162 of 1932-33; *A.R.E.* for 1932-33, pp. 65-66.
18. 146 of 1932-33; *A.R.E.* for 1932-33, pp. 65-66.
19. 166 of 1932-33.
20. 185 of 1894; *S.I.I.*, Vol. V, T.V. Mahalingam, *op. cit.*, p. 235.

Another inscription records a case of theft in the temple. According to this inscription, one Periyān was caught red-handed with the *tiruppattam* of the deity stolen by him from the temple. This case came before the assembly and he was ejected from his house as a *Śivadrōhin* and his house was confiscated and sold. The proceeds of the sale were utilised by the temple for paying the masons and the workers employed in the construction of the steps to the hundred-pillared hall in the temple.[21] The above two instances show that the properties of the *Śivadrōhins* did not escheat to the king but were made over to the temple.

TAXATION

Another important function of the *Sabhā* was to collect taxes, on behalf of the temple, on land and properties. In this connection it is of interest to note that an inscription records two kinds of taxes. One was *Peruvāram* or great share, which was generally one-sixth of the produce paid to the king. But it is not clear whether this tax was paid to the king, as the whole village was a *dēvadāna* to the temple. The second tax was *Śilavuvāram* (expenditure tax) which was probably a local cess levied to meet the expenses of the village in making repairs to tanks etc.[22]

Taxes were also levied by the *Sabhā* from the merchant communities, in favour of the temples, to meet the expenses of certain festivals. It is of interest to note that an inscription at Tirukkaḻukkuṉṟam states that several merchant communities of this place agreed to pay certain duties on their merchandise to the temple treasury to meet the expense of the *Tai* festival of the temple.[23] Another inscription records the levy of a consolidated tax called *Kaṭṭukkuttugai* from the *Kaikōḷas* (weavers) of Tirukkaḻukkuṉṟam on the cloths that were exported and imported from Paṭṭinam (the modern Sadras). They were exempted from paying certain taxes apart from the consolidated amount of 70 *paṇam* per year. The taxes thus exempted were:

21. 179 of 1894.
22. 179 of 1894; *I.A.*, XXI, p. 284.
23. 63 of 1909; *S.I.T.I., T.I,.* Vol. I, p. 464.

Paṭṭādai, Nūlāyam, Attaiccammadam, Perccammadam, Mada-viratti and *Adiyamadam.*[24] *Māśa-Vāriyam* or monthly tax was another tax collected from merchants. This was a specified impost on all articles of merchandise such as Muttuppārvai, Puḍavai-pārvai etc., paid to conduct a worship in the temple. The cesses were also specified as follows: 1/10 per cent on the sale of cloth, 3/20 per cent on the sale of oil etc., and 8/20 *paṇam* on each bundle of saries (*Pudavaikkaṭṭu*) sold.[25]

TEMPLE AND SOCIAL AND ECONOMIC LIFE OF THE PEOPLE

The temple was not only a source of religious inspiration but was also a powerful social and economic entity and greatly influenced the social and economic life of the people. In the social life of the people the temples in South India generally played the role of fortresses, treasuries, courts, parks, fairs, exhibition sheds and halls of learning and of amusement, besides being the centre of culture and fine arts. For instance, in South India great importance was attached to the development of education among the people and the temples acted as centres of learning. Some of the inscriptions available in some of the important temples in South India may well bring out the role of the temples in this field. Inscriptions at Tiruvoṟṟiyur record provisions made for the recitation and teaching of *Śivadharma* and *Siddhānta* in the temple.[26] Provision was also made for the maintenance of a hall in the temple at Tiruvoṟṟiyur in which grammar was taught. Another inscription at Tirumukkūḍal near Kāñci records the maintenance of a school and a hostel for studying Vedas and Śāstras.[27] Again, an inscription of Rājē-ndra I at Eṇṇāyiram in South Arcot district gives an interesting detail about the maintenance of a college for the study of Vedas.[28] Inscriptions from several temples like those at Sendalai[29] also show that they served as educational

24. 170 of 1932-33.
25. 173 of 1932-33; *A.R.E.* for 1932-33, p. 70.
26. *A.R.E.* for 1913, p. 110. K.V. Raman, *The Early History of Madras Region.*
27. *A.R.E.* for 1916, p. 118 ff.
28. 333 of 1917.
29. 63 of 1897.

institutions. The Kūram plates also record an endowment for the same purpose.[30] Temples also encouraged fine arts, especially music and dance. The inscriptions on music at Kuḍimiyāmalai,[31] and on Bharatanāṭya at Chidambaram[32] are eloquent testimony to the interest evinced by the people in these fine arts. The temples at Tirukkaḻukkuṉṟam were no exception to this and they have also played a leading part in the promotion and preservation of the culture and fine arts.

CENTRE OF ART AND ARCHITECTURE

Temples at Tirukkaḻukkuṉṟam also played a prominent part in the development of art and architecture and sculpture. The construction of numerous temples gave opportunity to the sculptors to exhibit their skill. But for the encouragement given by the temples this art would not have developed. The temples at Tirukkaḻukkuṉṟam are shining examples of the high dexterity achieved by the artisans in building vast and yet graceful structures. The sculptures in the *Orukal maṇḍpa* and in the niches of the *Tiruābaraṇa-kōṭṭaḍi* are remarkable artistic pieces and bear testimony to the skilled craftsmanship and abiding devotion to the subject at hand.

AN EMPLOYER

The role of the temple in the economic life of the people was also significant. It provided work and the means of livelihood for great number of people. The most detailed account of the number of people employed in the temple and the wages given to them, is given in the inscription of Tanjore.[33] The list includes *Śivabrāhmaṇas*, drummers, dancing masters, dancing girls, singers etc. The wages of employees were often reckoned in terms of lands. Two inscriptions at Tirukkaḻukkuṉṟam record the employment of *Śivabrāhmaṇas* in the temple. They were probably *arcakas* and they occupied an honoured position in the

30. *S.I.I.*, Vol. I, p. 47.
31. *Ep. Ind.*, XII, No. 28.
32. *A.R.E.* for 1913-14.
33. *S.I.I.*, II, No. 66.

them. This is a beautiful bronze image and may be dated to the Cōḷa times.

Over the sanctum, is a medium-sized (about 35 feet) *vimāna* in brick and mortar. The entire *vimāna* is covered by beautiful sculptures of stucco which lend unique charm of its own to the structure. That it is a late Cōḷa structure is clearly borne out by its typical pilasters, niches and also the style of the sculptures on the *vimāna*.

On the south side of the *vimāna*, in the first row, is the sculpture of Dakṣiṇāmūrti in the *Vyākhyāna mudrā*, with his disciples. To his right, is Rṣabhārūdar. In the second row, are the figures of Bhikṣāṭana and Ardhanāri. On the west side, at the top, is Somāskanda, locally called as Vedagirīśvara. Viṣṇu is represented in the second and third rows. On the north side, in the top row, is Brahmā in *Sukhāsana* pose, with beard. He is also represented as holding the usual *āyudhas*, like rosary and *kalaśa*. In the second row Śiva is represented in the form of Urdhvatāṇḍava and in the third row Brahmā is again represented in standing posture. Figures of atlantis supporting the superstructure are prominent on all the sides of the *Vimāna*.

ĒKAMBARANĀTHAR SHRINE (G.P. II, No. 3)

Adjoining the Vēdagirīśvara shrine, to its south, is a small and simple shrine for Ēkambaranātha depicted in the form of a huge linga. The shrine is simple and square in structure of 6' by 6'. It has a small, narrow entrance. The roof is like a thatched hut or *kūṭa-śālā*. The walls and the roof are plain.

ĀTMANĀTHA SHRINE (G.P. II, No. 4)

Further south is the small but lovely shrine dedicated to Ātmanātha. It is a well-executed Cōḷa structure, with plinth or *upapīṭha* being finely moulded. It has a square cella about 12 ft x 12 ft with an ardhamaṇḍapa in front, which is also of the same dimension. The shrine is about 12 ft in height and has no *vimāna*. There are well-cut niches, five in number, which are, however, empty. The Cōḷa date of the structure is confirmed by the epigraph on its plinth on the southern side.

MĀṆIKKAVĀCAKAR SHRINE (G.P. II, No. 2)

On the southeastern corner of the *prākāra*, is a small shrine for Māṇikkavācakar. It is a square structure of about 6' x 6'. The walls are plain. There is an inscription dated 1135 A.D. on the southern wall, which refers to the presence of the shrine at that time.[11]

VAṆḌUVANAPPIḶḶAIYĀR, JAMBUKEŚVARA & SUBRAHMAṆYA (Fig. 19)

On the southwestern corner of the *prākāra*, are the shrines of Vaṇḍuvanappiḷḷaiyār, Jambukeśvara and Subrahmaṇya. All the three shrines are of the same style, though of different sizes. They are evidently of the later Cōḷa period as is evidenced by the corbels of the pilasters as well as the style of the graceful stucco figures on the *vimānas*. The structures are simple, square or rectangular or plain, with *ardhamaṇḍapas*. Their walls are plain with no niches or sculptures. The height of the Vaṇḍuvanappiḷḷaiyār shrine is about 25 feet while the other two are about 15 feet in height. The *vimāna* of the Vaṇḍuvanappiḷḷaiyār has only representations of Vināyaka in various postures while the *vimāna* on the Subrahmaṇya shrine has representation of only Subrahmaṇya along with his consorts, Vaḷḷi and Dēvayāni.

ARUṆACALEŚVARA SHRINE (G.P. II, No. 8)

On the northeastern side of the *prākāra* is a very small shrine for Aruṇacaleśvarar in a linga form (Fig. 20). It is a rectangular structure having a Tējōlinga. There are two other lingas on either side of the entrance. The entrance is small and narrow.

TRIPURASUNDARI AMMAN SHRINE (G.P. II, No. 9)

By the side of the Aruṇacaleśvarar shrine, in the northwest corner of the *prākāra*, is the shrine dedicated to Tripurasundari Amman. It consists of a 20 feet square cella, an *antarāla* and a *mahāmaṇḍapa*. It is a fine later Cōḷa edifice. Its plinth or *upapītha* has moulded parts. The walls of the shrine have well-

11. 186 of 1932-33.

cut niches and pilasters having typical later Cōḷa corbels. There are two niches each on the south and north walls and one on the west wall. They are however empty. There are two inscriptions of the 9th year of Jaṭāvarman Sundara Pāṇḍya (1260 A.D.) on the west wall of the shrine. There is a covered verandah round the *pradakṣiṇā* of the shrine.

The deity is known as Tripurasundari or *Peṇṇinallāḷ*.[12] Remarkable grace and unique charm characterise the image of the goddess who has been the object of devotion and worship for many a century. Almost life-size, the image is awe-inspiring, and a veritable embodiment of dignified feminine beauty. She is depicted with four arms, the upper hands having flowers, while the lower hands are in the *abhaya* and *varada* poses. Her whole body is covered with silver plate.[13]

There is a *maṇḍapa* in front of this shrine with 40 ornamental pillars. Though it is a modern addition of the present century, its horse pillars and corbel designs are done in the Vijayanagara style.

PRATYAKṢA VEDAGIRĪŚVARA

On the east of the abovesaid *maṇḍapa*, there is a small shrine dedicated to Vedagirīśvara in the form of a linga. The shrine has a cella of about 6' square and a *mukhamaṇḍapa* of the same dimension. It has a *vimāna* of about 10' height. The walls are plain and simple.

RIṢI GŌPURA (G.P. and Fig. 21)

Before entering into the third and the outermost *prākāra*, we pass through an entrance with a *gōpura*, known as Riṣi Gōpura. The plinth of this *gōpura* is about 25 feet square while the *gōpura*

---

12. It is of interest to note that the *Dēvāram* hymnist Sambandar refers, in one of his verses in his *Padigam* on Tirukkaḻukkuṉṟam, to the Goddess, *Peṇṇinallāḷ*. He says,
துணையல் செய்தான் தூய வண்டியாழ் செய் சுடர்க் கொன்றை
பிணையல் செய்தான் பெண்ணினல்லாளை யொரு பாகம்... (verse 4)
13. It is said that this sculpture is so fragile that *abhiṣeka* is performed only thrice in a year on the Adi puram day, on the last day of Navarātri festival and on the Panguni Uttiram day.

is 35 feet high. The plinth is covered with numerous inscriptions, the earliest of which is dated in the 23rd year of Kulōttunga I (i.e. 1093 A.D.). The upper storeys are built of brick and mortar. The outer face of the *gōpura* is indented by numerous *kūḍus*, which are typical of the Cōḷa period, and are studded with many figures in stucco, depicting various forms of Śiva and other Gods like Vināyaka.

VINĀYAKA AND SUBRAHMAṆYA SHRINES

On the left side of the *Riṣi gōpura* is a small but lovely shrine dedicated to Vināyaka. This is a short one about 6 feet in height with round pillars and corbels typical of the later Cōḷa period. The sculpture is also a beautiful one of later Cōḷa date. On the right is the shrine dedicated to Subrahmaṇya, which is similar to that of the Vināyaka shrine.

GŌPURAS (Figs. 22 to 26)

Altogether there are four gateways to the Bhaktavatsala temple complex crowned by four lofty towers or gōpuras with the main entrance on the east. They lend special beauty and serve as prominent landmarks to the architectural layout of the temple and the town. All the four share many common architectural and decorative traits characteristic of the Vijayanagara-Nāyak style i.e. 16th-17th centuries. The general common features are: The stone basement (*adhiṣṭhāna*) is about 25 feet in height and carries ornamental niches, *Kumbapanjara* pilasters and a series of miniature Kūḍu-arches. Many of the niches have in them sculptures like Dvārapālakas (door-keepers), Gaṇēśa and Subrahmaṇya on either side of the main entrance and several other forms of Śiva like Gajasamhāra-m ūrti, Bhairava etc. The entrance doorway or threshold is flanked by the holy river goddesses Ganga and Yamuna holding creepers which go up in circular rings or coils upto the top. Inside these rings are shown miniature figures of divinities and saints or Śiva-lingas. Exquisite carvings with lotus design are found on the ceilings of the entrance corridor. In the ceiling of the North Gōpura, the eight directional deities (*aṣṭadikpālas*) are depicted in their appropriate quarters. In the ceiling of the West Gōpura, traces of old paintings depicting the Sthalapurana legends of the two eagles are found.

The brick superstructures over stone basements rise in several storeys or *talas* to an average height of about 40 to 50 feet. The total average height of the gōpuras from the ground level would be about 75 feet. The gōpura on the north is the tallest and has nine tiers or *talas* while the other three have seven *talas*. Each tier has a doorway flanked by doorkeepers (Dvārapālakas). Each tier is marked off with a row of miniature shrines (*mālika*) consisting of *kūṭas* (square plan), *panjaras* (apsidal) and *śālās* (rectangular). The towers are topped by a rectangular neck (*griva*) and a heavy *śālā-śikhara* and a row of seven or nine copper finials or *kalaśas*. We also see quite a few figures of Śaiva icons and other divinities in stucco on the body of the gōpuras. They have been renovated and painted over in the recent years. On the whole, the gōpuras of Tirukkaḷukkuṉṟam serve as impressive architectural landmarks of the temple town and also attest to the excellence attained in stone craftsmanship by our great sthapatis who combined in them deep devotion, knowledge of religious lore and age-old traditional skills. It is rather unfortunate that there are no records or inscriptions to tell us about the names of those master-architects and sculptors who designed and erected the *gōpuras, maṇḍapas* and the numerous sculptures. True devotees as they were, they chose to remain humble and anonymous.

ĀMAI MAṆḌAPA (Figs. 27 to 29)

In the southwest corner of the outer *prākāra* there is a beautifully designed *maṇḍapa* called Āmai-maṇḍapa with 60 tall and exquisitely carved pillars. Some pillars are ornamented with rearing horsemen, while others are with *yālis*. In the middle of this maṇḍapa, there is a platform designed like the back of a tortoise of Āmai, which is auspicious symbol of stability. Above the ceiling of this platform, Bhūtagaṇas in various postures are carved. There are two flights of steps, one each on the east and on the north, with beautifully carved *vyāli* balustrades. This Āmai maṇḍapa may be dated to the Vijaya-nagara-Nāyak period and it belongs to the class generally known as Kalyāṇa Maṇḍapas that became popular during the 16th to 18th centuries.

Apart from its architectural excellence, the Maṇḍapa is noteworthy for numerous relief sculptures on its pillars, depicting various forms of Śiva (like Naṭarāja), Gaṇeśa, Subrahmaṇya, Rāma, Goddess Lakṣmi, Cow and Elephant worshipping the Linga, saints and sages (like Vyāgrapāda).

SIXTEENPILLAR MAṆḌAPA

Another interesting structure in the temple is the sixteen-pillar Maṇḍapa on the southeastern side of the first enclosure. Here also we see some good sculptures like Dakṣi ṇām ūrti, Kaschayapa worshipping Linga, Pārvati in penance, Gaja-samhāramūrti, portraits of chieftains etc.

ILLUSTRATIONS (Figs. 30 to 47)

A list of selected sculptures illustrated in this volume and their location are given here. All are from the Bhaktavatsala Temple.

Dvārapālaka, Lingōdhbhava, Sūrya, Śaiva Nāyanmārs (all in the inner enclosure around the main sanctum), Gajasamhāra, Pārvati in penance (all in the sixteen-pillar maṇḍapa), river goddess Ganga, Śaiva saints or Nāyanmārs (southern gopura entrance) and Dikpālas on the ceiling (western gopura), Indra with elephant Airāvata, Agni with his vehicle ram, goddess Lakṣmi, sage Vyāgrapāda, elephant offering worship to the Linga, Cow pouring milk over the Linga (all from Āmai Mandapa), Durgā on a pillar, Śaiva saints (south gopura entrance), two eagles and the hill temple (inner enclosure).

BRONZES

The temple also has a number of beautiful bronze images of processional deities and saints. Two of them – Somaskanda and Naṭarāja of the Cōḷa period are illustrated here (Figs. 48 and 49).

APPENDIX I

A SELECT LIST OF INSCRIPTIONS FROM TIRUKKAḺUKKUṈṞAM, ARRANGED CHRONOLOGICALLY

DATE	KING	REFERENCE
	PALLAVAS	
–	Narasimha-varman I	65 of 1909; S.I.I. ,XII, No. 16; A.R.E. for 1932-33, p. 55
	CŌḶAS	
27th Year	Āditya I (871-907)	167 of 1894; E.I., III, p. 276
13th Year	Parāntaka I (907- 955 A.D.)	168 of 1894; E.I., III, p. 280
16th Year	Rājēndra I (1012-44)	171 of 1894; S.I.I., V, No. 464
5th Year	Rājēndra II (1052-64)	173 of 1894; S.I.I., V, No. 466
13th Year	" "	128 of 1932-33
7th Year	Vīrarajēndra I (1063-69)	175 of 1894; S.I.I., V, No. 468
14th Year	Kulōttunga I (1070-1120)	174 of 1894; S.I.I., III, No. 69
23rd Year	" "	180 of 1894

42nd Year	Vikramacōḷa	179 of 1894; S.I.I., No. 75; I.A., XXI, p. 281
47th Year	Kulōttunga I	124 and 137 of 1932-33
3rd Year	Vikramacōḷa (1118-1135)	176 of 1894; S.I.I., V, No. 469
" "	" "	139 of 1932-33
" "	" "	150 of 1932-33
		155 of 1932-33
4th Year	" "	154 of 1932-33
9th Year	" "	151 of 1932-33
13th Year	" "	152 of 1932-33
14th Year	" "	180 of 1932-33
" "	" "	177 of 1932-33
15th Year	" "	127 of 1932-33
3rd Year	Kulōttunga II (1133-1150)	140 of 1932-33
" "	" "	186 of 1932-33
" "	" "	142 of 1932-33
5th Year	" "	157 of 1932-33
6th Year	" "	162 of 1932-33
" "	" "	165 of 1932-33
9th Year	" "	138 of 1932-33
12th Year	" "	146 of 1932-33
" "	" "	183 of 1932-33
9th Year	Rājādhirāja II (1163-1179)	184 of 1932-33
12th Year	" "	159 of 1932-33
14th Year	" "	123 of 1932-33
20th Year	Kulōttunga III (1178-1216)	136 of 1932-33
24th Year	" "	133 of 1932-33
25th Year	" "	156 of 1932-33

25th Year	" "	163 of 1932-33; S.I.T.I., Vol. I
" "	" "	121 of 1932-33
30th Year	" "	153 of 1932-33
34th Year	" "	178 of 1932-33
35th Year	" "	149 of 1932-33
37th Year	" "	182 of 1894; S.I.I., V, No. 475
38th Year	" "	144 of 1932-33
" "	" "	145 of 1932-33
7th Year	Rājarāja III (1216-1246)	143 of 1932-33
9th Year	" "	129 of 1932-33
12th Year	" "	166 of 1932-33
17th Year	" "	158 of 1932-33
18th Year	" "	164 of 1932-33
20th Year	" "	131 of 1932-33
—	" "	161 of 1932-33

RĀṢṬRAKŪṬAS

17th Year	Krishṇa III (939-966)	169 of 1894; E.I., III, 282
19th Year	" "	170 of 1894

PĀṆḌYAS

9th Year	Jaṭāvarman Sundara (acc. 1251)	188 of 1894; I.A., XXI, p. 343; S.I.I., V, No. 482
" "	" "	187 of 1894; S.I.I.,V, No. 481
" "	" "	186 of 1894; S.I.I.,V, No. 480
15th Year	" "	147 of 1932-33

KĀḌAVARĀYAS

21st Year	Kōpperunjungadēva	181 of 1894; S.I.I.,V, No. 474
31st Year	" "	148 of 1932-33
34th Year	" "	160 of 1932-33

SAMBŪVARĀYAS

3rd Year	Rājanārāyaṇa Sambūvarāya (1337-1360)	178 of 1894; S.I.I., V, No. 471
10th Year	" "	61 of 1909; S.I.T.I., Vol. I

VIJAYANAGARA

1376 A.D.	Bukka I	173 of 1932-33; S.I.T.I., Vol. I
—	Vīra Kampaṇa II	185 of 1894
—	" "	170 of 1932-33
1388 A.D.	Virūppaṇa Uḍaiyar	171, 172, 174 and 175 of 1932-33; S.I.T.I., Vol. I
S. 1328	Bukka II	57 of 1909; S.I.T.I., Vol. I
S. 1328	" "	58 of 1909; S.I.T.I., Vol. I
—	Dēvarāya I	177 of 1894; S.I.I., V, No. 470
S. 1365	Dēvarāya II	176 of 1932-33.
A.D. 1519	Krishnadēvarāya	130 of 1932-33

B. UNDATED INSCRIPTIONS

184 of 1894

189 of 1894; S.I.I., V, No. 484

59 of 1909; S.I.T.I., Vol. I, p. 463

63 of 1909; S.I.T.I., Vol. I, p. 464

64 of 1909; S.I.T.I., Vol. I, p. 465

66 to 73 of 1909

329(a) to (m) of 1911

330, 331 of 1911

122, 125, 126, 134, 135, 141, 167, 168, 169, 179, 181, 182, 185, 188 to 191 of 1932-33

C. SOME TEMPLE RECORDS IN THE ORIENTAL MSS. LIBRARY, MADRAS

D. No.	3182	D. No.	2771
" "	3183	" "	2772
" "	3768	" "	2773
" "	3766	R. No.	1618
" "	3767	" "	1619
" "	3770	" "	1620

APPENDIX II

BRIEF ABSTRACTS OF INSCRIPTIONS OF TIRUKKAḶUKKUṈṘAM AS GIVEN IN THE EPIGRAPHICAL REPORTS FOR THE YEARS 1894, 1910 AND 1911

167 of 1894 (Tamil). On the wall of the strong room of the Bhaktavatsala I Temple. A record of the Chola King Ko-Rajakesarivarman (Aditya I) dated in his twenty-seventh year, renewing a grant made by the Pallava kings Skandasishya and Vatapikonda Narasimhavarman. See *Madras Christian College Magazine* for October 1890, and *Ep. Ind.*, III, 277-80. Mr. Venkayya identifies Narasimha with Narasimhavarman I, the contemporary of Gnanasambanda and Siruttonda.

168 of 1894 (Tamil). On the same wall. A record of the Chola king Madirakonda Ko-Parakesarivarman (i.e., Parantaka I) in his thirteenth year. Records gift of a lamp by Nedumal Sattan Sennipperayan of Karaikkattur in Amur-kottam and his mother. See *Ep. Ind.*, III, 280-1.

169 of 1894 (Tamil). On the same wall. A record of the Rashtrakuta king Kannaradeva (Krishna III), dated in his seventeenth year. Published by Mr. Venkayya in *the Madras Christian Magazine* for April 1892, and *Ep. Ind.*, III, pp. 282-6., Records gift of lamp by a native of Karai.

170 of 1894 (Tamil). On the same wall. A record of the Rashtrakuta king Kannaradeva, dated in his nineteenth year. Records that a Sattan of Karai built a hall in the shrine and provided for water, fire, etc., besides one *patti* of land which he had purchased from Isana Siva or Nakkadi Bhatta. The money was deposited with the local Sabha.

171 of 1894 (Tamil). On the same wall. A record of the Chola king Ko-Parakesarivarman *alias* Rajendra Chola I (1012-43) in his sixteenth year. Gift of a lamp.

172 of 1894 (Tamil). On the same wall. Records in the twenty-sixth year of the Chola King Ko-Rajakesarivarman *alias* Rajadhirajadeva gift of land. (The King was very probably Rajadhiraja I who ruled from 1018 to 1052.)

173 of 1894 (Tamil). On the same wall. Records in the fifth year of the Chola King Ko-Parakesarivarman *alias* Rajendradeva (1052-63) gift of land.

174 of 1894 (Tamil). On the same wall. Records in the fourteenth year of the Chola King Rajakesarivarman *alias* Kulottunga-Choladeva (1070-1118) gift of 90 ewes for a lamp. See. *S.I.I.,* III, No. 69, pp. 143-8.

175 of 1894 (Tamil). On the same wall. Records in the third year of the Chola King Vikrama Choladeva (1118-35) gift of a lamp.

176 of 1894 (Tamil). On the same wall. Records in the third year of the Chola King Vikrama Choladeva (1118-35) gift of a lamp.

177 of 1894 (Tamil). On the east wall of the second *prakara* of the same temple, right of entrance. A damaged record of the Vira-Devaraya Udaiyar dated Vikriti.

178 of 1894 (Tamil). On the same wall. Records in the third year of Raja Narayana Samburaya (i.e., A.D. 1340) gift of a lamp.

179 of 1894 (Tamil). On the south wall of the *prakara*. A record of the Chola King Ko-Rajakesarivarman *alias* Kulottunga-Choladeva I, dated in his forty-second year. Records that an inhabitant of Rajarajapuram made over 10 *kasu* to temple authorities who purchased with this some land for maintaining a *matha* of Naminandi Adigal and one of the 63 devotees of Siva. *S.I.I.,* III, No. 75, pp. 164-8, also *Ins. S. Dis.,* p. 169, No. 6 and *Ind. Antq.,* Vol. XXI, p. 281-ff.

180 of 1894 (Tamil). On the same wall. Records in the twenty third year of the Chola King Ko-Rajakesarivarman *alias* Kulottunga-Choladeva a copy of a former copper-plate recording the boundaries of Tirukkaḷukkuṉṟam. This inscription is given in *Ins. S. Dis.,* p. 170, No. 8, but the year is given as 33.

181 of 1894 (Tamil). On the same wall, Ko-Perunjingadeva records in his twenty-first year gift of a lamp. See *Ep. Ind.,* VII,

165. The date corresponded, according to Kielhorn, to Saturday, the 10th February, A.D. 1274.

182 of 1894 (Tamil). On the same wall. A record of Tribhuvanaviradeva (i.e., Kulottunga III (1178-1216) in his thirty-seventh year relating gift of lamp.

183 of 1894 (Tamil). On the west wall of the same *prakara*. An incomplete record of the Chola King Ko-Parakesarivarman *alias* Rajadhirajadeva (II?), dated in his ninth year. Records gift of a lamp.

184 of 1894 (Tamil). On the same wall. Gift of land by Konerimaikondan in his thirty-fourth year, for repairs of the temple.

185 of 1894 (Tamil). On the inside of the east wall of third *prakara* of the same temple, right of entrance. A damaged record of Kampana-Udaiyar (II?), son of Vira (Bukka I?) dated Ananda. This is evidently Inscription No. 22, in *Ins, S. Dis.,* p. 174, No. 22. It says that the property of the deity stolen by a man was restored at the expense of his own, worth 750 *panams.*

186 of 1894 (Tamil). On the west wall of the Tripurasundari shrine in the same temple. Records in the ninth year of the Pandya King Ko-Jatavarman *alias* Sundara Pandyadeva I (1251-6) gift of a lamp. See *Ep. Ind.,* VI, 307, where Kielhorn points out that the exact date is Sunday, 15th June, A.D. 1259. See *Ins. S. Dis.,* p. 173, No. 19, where the regnal year is misread as 1.

187 of 1894 (Tamil). On the same wall. Records in the ninth year of the Pandya King Ko-Jatavarman *alias* Sundara-Pandyadeva (1251-64) gift of gold. *Ind. Antq.*, XXI, 343. See the Srirangam and Tiruppukkuli inscriptions, *Ind. Antq.,* XXII, p. 221 and *Ep. Ind.,* VI, p. 307, where Kielhorn gives the date as Tuesday, 29th April, 1259. See also *Ins. S. Dis.,* p. 173, No. 20.

188 of 1894 (Tamil). On both sides of the entrance into the second *prakara* of the same temple. Records in the ninth year of the Pandya King Sundara Pandyadeva.

64 of 1909 (Tamil). In the same place. Records in the reign of the Vijayanagara King Bhupatiraya, in S. 1330, gift of 32 cows for a lamp by a native of Nerkulam, at the rate of $\frac{1}{4}$ measure of ghee daily for a lamp. See *Ins. S. Dis.,* p. 172, No. 15 also. (Bhupati was son of Bukka II.)

65 of 1909 (Tamil). At the top of the second pillar from the right in the upper verandah of the *Orukal Mandapa*, on the hill. A damaged record. Mentions Kalatturkottam, Mulatanattu Perumanadigal and Vatapikonda Narasingapottarasa (i.e., Narasimhavarman I, the conqueror of Vatapi). *S.I.I.*, XII, No. 16.

66 to 73 of 1909 (English). On the eight pillars of upper and lower verandah in the same *mandapa*. Records in seventeenth century A.D. signatures of Dutch officers.

74 of 1909 (English). On the walls of the same *mandapa*. Records in the seventeenth century A.D. signatures of Dutch officers.

75 of 1909 (English). At the entrance into one of the temple kitchens of the same hill. Records signatures of Dutch officers of the nineteenth century.

329 (*a*) to (*m*) of 1911 (Roman characters). On the wall at the entrance into the birds' kitchen, on the hill. The following names (read tentatively) are engraved:

(*a*) A.D. Kiegr 1-m i-d 1666; (*b*) C.J. Keys, Price, ... Gyfford; (*c*) ... H.C. Rabel, 89 Alack, L Gray... Anne; (*d*) H. Dubon 1749; (*e*) ... vkerck; (*f*) T. Campic ...; (*g*) D.V.A.S.; (*h*) J.A. Van Braam Nederld Commiss XX Febry MDCCCXIII, C-40 I S. Peelman; (*i*) N.D. Jong Heere 1749; (*j*) 85. T. Poughion, 35; (*k*) P.E. Van Hogendrop A. Vandenbroek (see Cotton's *Tombs*, p. 187, No. 1006), A.M.E.L. Brachi 1793, M. Dormx, Wed. L Alag ... C.W. Cantervisscher 179 ...; (*l*) W. Van Somesan ...; P. St. Paul C.J. Keveseeg, 1750, C.P. Keller; (*m*) Lucas, L. Hemsinck ... 8-m 13-d 1662. The last was either the chief of Sadraspatam from A.D. 1666 to 1686 or an engineer of that name who died in 1661. See *Ep. Rep.*, 1912, 92 for details.

330 of 1911 (Roman characters). On the wall of the temple kitchen of the same hill. Perhaps damaged at the right end. Registers the names: W. Silves H. Stee ... 5.

331 of 1911 (Roman characters). On the west wall of a ruined *mandapa* in the North Main Street of the same village. "Geo: Dawson lived in this Choy Fm. 18th October to 9th December, 1769." Dawson was a Madras Civilian entered the company's

service in 1751. Member of Madras Council, 1768, Chief of Cuddalore, 1769. Returned to England, 1776. See *Ep. Rep.*, 1912, p. 92.

On the south wall of the gate in the temple of Bhakta-vatsalasvami. Records that one Tondamana Rayan purchased the village "Echencaurana" for 250 golden *panams* and granted it to the God in Vibhava. *Ins. Ced. Dis.*, p. 151, No. 1.

In the same place. Records that one Narayanadeva and another gave, in the reign of Virupanna Udaiyar, the village of Vampattu (1) for 1360 *panams*. *Ibid.*, No. 2. The setting up of a linga by a chief of Adigal and gift of $67\frac{1}{2}$ *panams*. See *Ins. S. Dis.*, p. 174, No. 21, where this inscription is given.

189 of 1894 (Tamil). On the south wall of the Bhaktavatsala temple. A much-damaged record of the Pandya King Sundara Pandya.

57 of 1909 (Tamil). On the north wall of the kitchen in the Bhaktavatsaleswara temple, left of entrance. The Vijayanagara King Virapratapa Bukkaraya II records in S. 1328, Vyaya, gift of land for repairs and for the festival called Bukkarayan-sandi (named after the king), to the temple of Tirukkalukkunra-mudaiya Nayanar. See *Ins. S. Dis.*, p. 171, No. 10.

58 of 1909 (Tamil). In the same place. Dated in the reign of the Vijayanagara King Pratapa Bukkaraya II. Records in S. 1328, Vyaya, gift of land to the temple of Tirumalai Aludaiya Nayanar, by the people of Ayinavellipparu. See *Ins. S. Dis.*, p. 171, No. 11, where this inscription is given.

59 of 1909 (Tamil). In the same place. A damaged record of the Pandya King Jatavarman *alias* Tribhuvanachakravartin Vira Pandyadeva, dated 13th year. Records gift of a village for the festival called Kalingarayan-sandi to the same temple by the inhabitants of Kalattur-parru. Tirukkalukkunram was a village in Kalattur-kottam in Jayangondacholamandalam. Mentions Kappalur *alias* Ulagalandasolanallur in Mutturukkuram in Pandi-mandalam. (The king came to the throne in 1253 and so the year of the inscription was A.D. 1266. This inscription is given in the *Mack MSS.*) See *Ins. S. Dis.*, p. 172, No. 13.

60 of 1909 (Tamil). In the same place. A damaged record of the

Vijayanagara King Virapratapa Devaraya, dated in S. 1320, Paridhavi. (This inscription is given in the *Mack MSS*. It is said to record the grant of Vangalapakam to Tirukkalukkunra Nayanar.) See *Ins. S. Dis.*, p. 171, No. 12.

61 of 1909 (Tamil). On the same wall, right of entrance. Records in the tenth year of Sakalalokachakravartin Rajanarayana Sambuvaraya (i.e., A.D. 1347) gift of land, by purchase, to the temple of Tirukkalukkunramudaiya Nayanar. Mentions Pudupattinam *alias* Solamarttandanallur in Mondur-nadu, a sub-division of Amurkottam, a district of Jayangondachola-mandalam, See *Ins. S. Dis.*, p. 172, No. 16. It says that the village was worth 350 *panams*.

62 of 1909 (Tamil). In the same place. Records in the seventh year of the Pandya King Maravarman *alias* Tribhuvanachakravartin Vikrama-Pandyadeva gift of cows for a lamp to the shrine of Shanmukha-pillaiyar by a native of Vanavanadevi-chatturvedimangalam in Amurkottam. (This king is identical with that Maravarman Vikrama Pandya who came to the throne in 1282, and who was the victor over Viragandagopala and Ganapati of the Kakatiya dynasty.

63 of 1909 (Tamil). In the same place. Records in the reign of the Vijayanagara King Vira-Vijaya Bhupatiraya (Bukka III) gift of taxes for a festival by Nagesvaramudaiyan Villavarayan who was the agent of the king. See *Ins. S. Dis.*, p. 172, No. 14.

On the south wall of the gate of Bhaktavatsala temple. Records that in the same reign in Vibhava, 53 *Velis* in a village were sold for 1,560 *panams. Ibid.*, No. 3.

In the same place. Records that Vira Kampana Udaiyar levied on the local weavers a tax of 70 *panams* per annum, to be paid to the deity. *Ibid.*, No. 4.

On the eastern wall of the gate of the kitchen in the Bhaktavatsala shrine. Records in the shrine of Devaraya the sale of $3\frac{3}{4}$ *karai* of land at Kottappakkam for 820 *panams* and its endowment to the deity. *Ibid.*, p. 173, No. 17.

On the north prakara wall. Records that Tiruvenkattu Udaiyan granted 550 *kulis* of land to the deity in twenty-first year of Tribhuvanaviradeva (Kulottunga III). *Ibid.*, p. 173,

No. 18.

On a stone in the tank of Sankhu-tirtham. Records that Kulottunga-Choladeva granted in his third year 32 *velis* of land in the village of Kulottunga-Chola-Nellore. *Ibid.*, p. 875, No. 23.

In the prakara of the temple on the top of the hill. Records that a certain chief erected the *mandapam* in front of the Vedagiriswami temple. *Ibid.*, p. 175, No. 24.

On the south wall of the inner temple. Records the presentation of a jewel to the God by a private person. *Ibid.*, p. 176, No. 25.

On a gate step of the Vinayaka temple in the southern wall of Vedagirisvarar temple. Records that one Suryadeva of Puvinur village erected the steps to ascend the hill and the pagoda of Vinayaka. *Ibid.*, p. 176, No. 26.

On the western wall of the *mandapam* of the Amman shrine. Records the gift of the village of Amaranputtur for the *Avani festival* by the inhabitants of a village to God Adichandresvara. *Ibid.*, p. 177, No. 27.

RUDRANKOIL

At a distance of a few furlongs stands the village of Rudrankoil, where Siva is said to have fought with several *Asuras* or demons and gained a victory over them. There is now an ancient Siva temple at the spot.

VISIT OF THE DUTCH

Several Dutch gentlemen have visited this hill and their signatures are seen over the pillars of the *mandapa* on the hill. The following signatures relating to them are detailed in the report of the Madras Government Epigraphist for the year 1908-09:

"L. Hemeinck

De E. Hr. Ant. Pavilion

Johs. H. (u) yemn

(d) Ha. (r) t

A. (D). Klerck
L. Hemsinck De Jonge
Pieter Hemsinck
H. Helene (H)emsing
Heussen
Amarentia Hemsinck
Joannes Blockhevins
Martinus Pit
Marten Pit
Jacomina Baffart
Wilhenuna Dinker
Johana Duicker
D(e) (E.) W.C. Hartsink
De Wit
J. Corbisier
Wm. Groenege (u) s
Laurens Pit D'(j)onge
Helene Dinker

The signatures in Roman characters engraved on the pillars of the *Orukal-mandapa* on the Tirukkalukkunram hill bear dates below them, ranging between A.D. 1664 and 1687. Of these De E. (Edele) Hr. (Heer) Ant. (Anthoni) Pavilioen (i.e., the Honourable Mr. Anthony Pavilioen) whose name is inscribed on the east face of the second pillar in the upper verandah of the cave, was evidently from the title "Edelle" which was given only to the Governors of the Coromandal Coast or to members of their Council, a personage of high position. Some interesting details about him are given in Valentyn's *"Onu en Nieum Oost Indien"*. He was the chief at Masulipatam in A.D. 1658 and the commander (chief) at Jaffna in A.D. 1661. He appears to have continued in this latter position till 1st September, 1665, when he was appointed Governor of Coromandal and held that high position at Pulicat for 13 years from 10th October, 1665 to 1676. He was made an extraordinary member of the Batoia Council in A.D. 1668 and an ordinary member in 1676. His Excellency perhaps visited Sadras in 1670 and on his way paid a visit to the hill at Tirukkalukkunram from Tirupolur which was along the inland route from Sadraspatam to Pulicat. Tirupolur, which is stated by Valentyn to contain a "beautiful heathen temple", must be the modern Tirupporur, about 7 miles north-east of Tirukkalukkunram. A memoir drawn up by Anthony Pavilioen on the eve of his departure from Jaffnapatam has been printed at the end of the book entitled "Memoirs and Instructions of Dutch Governors, Commanders, etc.", published by the Ceylon Government. Johs. (i.e., Jodannes) Pavilioen (5) is probably to be identified with the son of the Honourable Anthony Pavilioen and he is the second in the factory at Negapatam from 1672 to 1673.

Laurens Pit D'Jonge (Lawrence Pit Junior) was another of the Governors of the coast from 1687 to 1698. He was born in India and perhaps visited Sadras in the company of Laurens Pit Senior (Governor of the coast from 1652 to 1663) while he was yet young and took a pleasure trip to the Tirukkalukkunram hill. Before becoming Governor he was the Chief of Masulipatam from 1685 to 1687 and in that capacity went in 1686 on an embassy to Golconda. He took Pondicherry from French and signed the articles of capitulation in 1693.

De E (delc) W.C. Hartsink, whose signature is on the east face of the pillar in the lower verandah, must be identified with Willem Carel Hartsink who was born in Japan on the 12th July, 1638, and was the chief merchant and President at Pulicat from 1679 to 1681. Hartsink was the second at Draksharamam in the Godavari District from 1660 to 1663 and the Chief of the Golconda factory from 1663 to 1677. In 1668, however, he appears as the second at Masulipatam. He occupied the position of the Chief at Masulipatam from 1677 till 1679 when he was appointed the chief merchant and, pending the appointment of a Governor, President at Pulicat. He returned to Masulipatam in 1681, retired from the service in 1685 and died in Holland on the 22nd May, 1689. A few lines below the signature of this gentleman, a passage in Tamil registers respect paid (evidently to the god Siva in the cave) by a certain Virakuvan of Palavakkattu, which is, perhaps, a variant of Palaverkkadu, the old name of Pulicat. Virakuvan (*i.e.*, Vira Ragavan) may have been a follower from Pulicat of the Hon'ble W.C. Hartsink.

Martinus Pit has probably to be identified with another son of the elder Pit. In 1674 he signed the articles of capitulation by the French at St. Thome. He was born at Pulicat and served for many years on the coast. Before 1675 he was the chief merchant of Devanampatam and from 1675 to 1677 he appears to have been the chief merchant at Pulicat and second-in-council. Perhaps in this latter capacity he went in 1675 to Batavia with a letter from Anthony Pavilioen, Governor of the Coromandal Coast, and on 12th July, 1676, returned in charge of three ships from Batavia. In 1677 he appears to have been called again to Batavia in consequence of a misunderstanding which he had with the then Governor of the Coromandal and was at Batavia on the 11th November, 1677. He was still in Batavia in 1678 and attended there the funeral of the Governor General on the 7th January, 1678. On the 3rd October in the same year he was appointed Visitateur General (Accountant General). His career henceforward appears to have been in Batavia where he stayed as an ordinary member of council from 1683 to 1690.

L. Hemsinck was the under-merchant and chief at Sadraspatam from A.D. 1666 to 1686. His appointment is dated 28th May, 1666. The wife of Lambert Hemsinck was Amarentia Hemsinck nee Blockhovisu whose tomb at Sadras is described on page 198 of Mr. Cotton's *Tombs*.

These signatures here signify the visit to this hill of many Dutch people among whom were Governors and Chiefs of Settlements. The summit of the hill commandng from its height a fine view of the plain below, right up to the sea-shore at Mahabalipuram, must have attracted the attention of the Dutch factors who frequently travelled between Pulicat and Sadras by way of Tirupporur. There is an illustration of the hill in "Havart" who himself visited it on the 3rd January, 1681."

APPENDIX III

TEXTS OF SOME INSCRIPTIONS

1. Inscription of Pallava King Vātāpikoṇḍa Narasimhavarman (I) found in the cave temple (Orukal Mandapa) at Tirukkaḷukkuṉṟam.

1. ஸ்ரீ திருக்கழுக்குன்றத்து பெருமாள்
2. அடிகளுக்கு களத்தூர் கோட்டத்து
3. திருக்கழுக்குன்றத்து
4. ஸ்ரீமலை மேல்
5. மூலத்தானத்து பெருமான்
6. அடிகளுக்கு வழிபாட்டுப் புறமாக
7. வாதாபி கொண்ட நரசிங்கப்
8. போத்தரசர் வைத்தது.

TRANSLATION

To the glorious God (Perumānaḍigaḷ) of Tirukkaḷukkuṉṟam: This (is the gift) made by Narasingapōttarasar who took Vatāpi (Badami) for worship (vaḷipāṭṭupuram) to the God (Perumānaḍigaḷ) of Mūlasthāna on the Sacred Hill (Srīmalai) at Tirukkaḷukkuṉṟam in ... Kaḷathūr-Kōṭṭam.

(Reference: 65 of 1909 and Annual Report of Epigraphy for 1932-33, p. 55 and *S.I.I.*, XII, No. 16)

2. Inscription of Rajakesarivarman (Aditya Chola I) on the wall of Sri Mūlasthanattu Udaiyar shrine, now called Thiruābharana-Kottadi in the Bhakthavatsala Temple at Tirukkaḷukkunram (167 of 1894; *Ep. Ind.*, III, pp. 277-80).

ஸ்வஸ்திஸ்ரீ கோ இராஜகேசரி பரம்மார்க்கு யாண்டு இருபத்தேழாவது களத்தூர் கோட்டத்துண் கூற்று திருக்கழுக்குன்றத்து ஸ்ரீ மூலஸ்தானத்து பெருமான் அடிகளுக்கு இறையிலியாக ஸ்கந்த சிஷ்யன் குடுத்தமைப்

படியே வாதாவி கொண்ட நரசிங்கப்போத்தரையிரும் அப்பரிசே ரக்ஷித்தமையில் அண்டுறையன் குணவன் மகன் புத்தன் விண்ணப்பத்தினால் பூர்வ ராஜாக்கள் வைத்தபடியே வைத்தேன் - இராஜகேசரிப்பரமன் இத் தர்மம்ரக்ஷித்தான் அடி என் முடி மேலின

TRANSLATION

Hail! Prosperity! In the twenty-seventh year (of the reign) of King Rājakēsarivarman whereas Skandasiṣya had given (certain land) free from taxes to the feet of the God of the holy Mūlasthāna (temple) at Tirukkaḷukkuṉṟam in Kalathūr-Kōṭṭam (and) in the sub-division called after itself (and) as accordingly, Narasingappōttaraiyar, the conqueror of Vātāpi, had confirmed (the grant) in the same manner. I Rājakēsari-varman at the request of Puttan, the son of Gunavan of Andurai have maintained (the grant) as the former Kings had maintained it.

The feet of one who protects this charity shall be on my head!

BIBLIOGRAPHY

1. CONTEMPORARY SOURCES

Annual Reports of Archaeological Survey of India.
Annual Reports of South Indian Epigraphy.
Archaeological Survey of India, South Indian Inscriptions.
Archaeological Survey of India, List of Antiquarian Remains in the Presidency of Madras, R. Sewell, 2 Vols.
Annual Reports of the Archaeological Department, Southern Circle (1882-1884).
Topographical List of Inscriptions of Madras Presidency, by V. Rangacharya, Vol. I (1919).
Epigraphia Indica.
South Indian Temple Inscriptions,
Edited by T.N. Subramanian, Vol. I (1953).

2. PURĀṆAS AND POETICAL COMPOSITIONS

Tirukkaḻukkuṉṟa Purāṇam, by Viraraghava Mudaliar.
Tirukkaḻukkuṉṟa-Ulā, by Viraraghava Mudaliar. Edited by U.V. Swaminatha Iyer.
Tirukkaḻukkuṉṟa-Mālai.
Kaḻugāsala Sadagam.
Tirukkaḻukkuṉṟa-Kōvai, by R. Somasundara Pillai.
Tirukkaḻukkuṉṟa Slēḍai Veṇba, by Sabapati Mudaliar.
Tirukkaḻukkuṉṟattandādi.
Malaimarunduppadigam.
Vēdagirīśvarar Padigam,
by Tirupporur Chidambaram Swamigal.

3. LITERARY WORKS

Tēvāram
Peria Purāṇam
Perumbāṇāṟṟupaḍai
Puranānūru
Tiruppugaḻ
Tiruvāsagam

4. MODERN WORKS

Anavaradavinayakam Pillai : *Tamiḻ Perumakkal Varalāru* (Tamil, 1921).

Appadurai, A. : *Economic Condition of Southern India, 1000-1500 A.D.*, 2 volumes (1936).

Arokiaswamy, M. : *History of the Vellar Basin* (1954).

Brown, Percy : *Indian Architecture* (Hindu).

Crole, C.S. : *Chingleput District Manual* (1879).

Dikshitar, V.R.R. : *Studies in Tamil Literature and History* (1936).

Dubreuil, J. : *Pallava Antiquities* (1916).

" : *The Pallavas* (1917)

" : *The Dravidian Architecture.*

" : *Iconography of South India.*

Fergusson, J. : *History of Indian and Eastern Architecture,* 2 volumes.

Gopalan, R. : *The History of the Pallavas of Kāñchi.*

Gopinatha Rao : *Elements of Hindu Iconography*, 2 volumes.

Heras, Rev. : *The Aravidu Dynasty of Vijayanagar.*

Jagadisa Aiyer, T.V. : *South Indian Shrines.*

Jagadisa Aiyer, T.V. : *South Indian Festivities.*

Kanakasabhai Pillai, V. : *The Tamils Eighteen Hundred Years Ago.*

Krishnaswami Iyengar, S. : *The Beginnings of South Indian History.*

" : *Evolution of Hindu Administrative Institutions* (1931).

Longhurst, A.H. : *Pallava Architecture (Memoirs of Archaeological Survey of India, No. 17).*

Love, H.D. : *Vestiges of Old Madras,* 4 volumes.

Mahalingam, T.V. : *Administration and Social Life under Vijayanagar.*

Mahalingam, T.V. : *South Indian Polity* (1955).

Minakshi, C. : *Administration and Social Life under the Pallavas* (1939).

Narayana Iyer, C.V. : *Origin and the Early History of Saivism in South India* (1936).

Nilakanta Sastri, K.A. : *The Cōḷas.*

\- : *Studies in Cōḷa History and Administration* (1932).

\- : *A History of South India* (1955).

\- : *The Pāṇḍyan Kingdom* (1929).

Nilakanta Sastri and Venkataramanayya : *Further Sources of Vijayanagar History,* 3 vols. (1946).

Pillay, K.K. : *Sucindram Temple* (1953).

Raman, K.V. : *Srivaradarajaswami Temple, Kanchi* (1975).

Raman, K.V. : *Early History of the Madras Region* (1959).

Satyanathier, R. : *Studies in the Ancient History of Tondaimaṇḍalam* (1944).

Satyanathier, R. : *The Nayaks of Madura.*

Sethu Pillai, R.P. : *Ūrum Pērum* (1946).

Sewell, R. : *A Forgotten Empire.*

: *Historical Inscriptions of Southern India,* Edited by S.K. Iyengar.

Sivaraja Pillai, K.N. : *Chronology of the Early Tamils.*

Srinivasa Aiyengar, M. : *Tamil Studies.*

Srinivasa Aiyengar, P.T. : *History of the Tamils from the Earliest Times to 600 A.D.*

Srinivasa Aiyengar, P.T. : *The Pallavas.*

Srinivasachari, C.S. : *History of the City of Madras.*

Srinivasachari, C.S. : *History of Gingee and its Rulers.*

Srinivasan, K.R. : *Temples of South India,* 1993.

Srinivasan, K.R. : *Cave Temples of Pallavas.*

Srinivasan, T.N. : *Handbook of South Indian Images.*

Subramaniam, K.R. : *The Origin of Saivism and its History in the Tamil Land.*

Subramaniya Iyer, K.V. : *Historical Sketches of the Ancient Deccan.*

Venkataraman, K.R. : *Hoysā las in the Tamil Country.*

Venkataramanayya, N. : *Origin of the South Indian Temples.*

Studies in the Third Dynasty of Vijayanagar.

5. JOURNALS

Ancient India

Indian Antiquary

Journal of Indian History

Journal of Mythic Society (Quarterly)

Kalaikkaḷañjiyam

Madras Journal of Literature and Science

Madras Christian College Magazine

Sen Tamil

INDEX

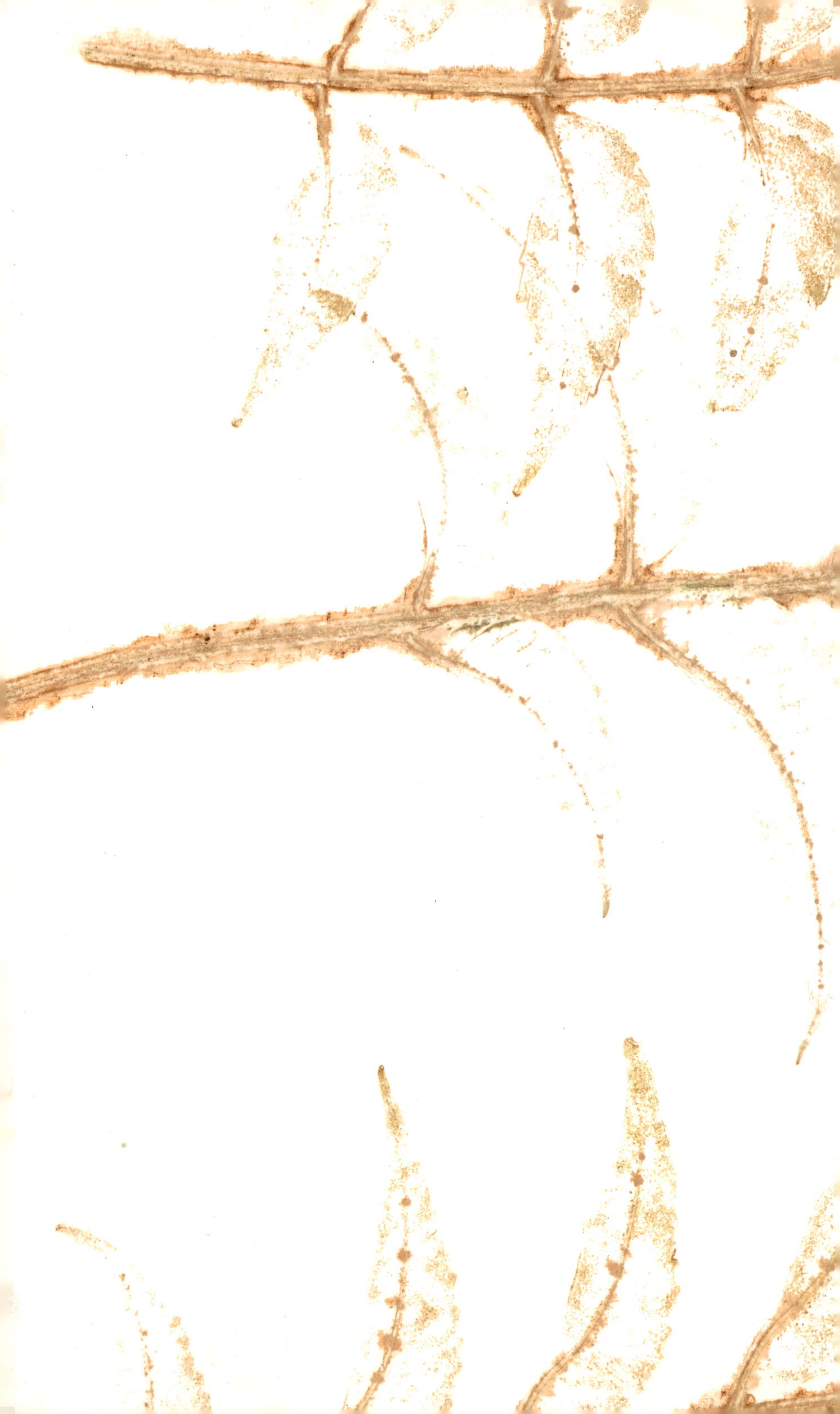